Working the American Way

How to communicate successfully with Americans at work

ROBERT DAY

howtobooks

Published by How To Books Ltd,
3 Newtec Place, Magdalen Road,
Oxford OX4 1RE. United Kingdom.
Tel: (01865) 793806. Fax: (01865) 248780.
email: info@howtobooks.co.uk
http://www.howtobooks.co.uk

First published 2004

British Library Cataloguing in Publication Data
A catalogue record for this book is available from the British Library

Cover design by Baseline Arts Ltd, Oxford
Produced for How To Books by Deer Park Productions, Tavistock
Typeset by PDQ Typesetting, Newcastle-under-Lyme, Staffs.
Printed and bound in Great Britain by Baskerville Press, Salisbury, Wiltshire

NOTE: The material contained in this book is set out in good faith for general guidance and no liability
can be accepted for loss or expense incurred as a result of relying in particular circumstances on
statements made in the book. The laws and regulations are complex and liable to change, and readers
should check the current position with the relevant authorities before making personal arrangements.

Contents

Acknowledgements

A few words of thanks are due here to a number of people who, directly or indirectly, have helped to bring the longstanding idea of writing a book about America to tangible reality:

Jeff Toms of Farnham Castle, and Farnham's clients from around the world whose search for knowledge about working with Americans has added so much to my own;

Helen Stiven and Derek Manuel of Hitachi Data Systems, who first gave me the opportunity to live and work in Britain and Europe, and to see America from a European viewpoint;

My teachers and friends who helped me learn about America: the late Dr. Willard Wallace of Berlin, Connecticut and Wesleyan University – who one evening several years ago, during a conversation around his kitchen table, said "Why don't you put this in a book?" – and Herbert Goodrow of Berlin High School.

My parents Ruth and Arthur Day for a lifetime of love and encouragement;

Those who assisted me with their opinions, experiences and information: Allen Cary of Belmont California, Sarah Day of New York City, Melanie Wentz Long of Oakland California, and Cathleen Avila of Houston Texas.

Most of all, to my wife Amilia for her patience, editorial comments, and extensive research and technical assistance, and to both her and our daughter Nor Aimy for holding up a Malaysian mirror to this American every day.

So it's home again, and home again,
America for me.
My heart is turning home again, and
There I long to be.

Henry Van Dyke, "America for Me"

EDITORIAL NOTE

To help you get used to one small aspect of the American way of business, throughout this book we have used American spelling, punctuation and usage, with one exception. Contrary to what Americans themselves might prefer, when referring to an unnamed or indefinite person, male or female, we use the third person masculine singular pronouns "he" and "him", rather than "he or she" and "him or her". We have more to say about this usage in Chapter 9, but we feel that the masculine singular is both more concise and smoother. That's something Americans will appreciate.

Farnham Castle International Briefing & Conference Centre

A lack of cultural understanding and local practices can be a major obstacle to the effectiveness of conducting business in another country. The ability to relate quickly and effectively with colleagues and clients in a new country is very important to long term success.

Farnham Castle International Briefing and Conference Centre is widely acknowledged as the world's leading provider of intercultural management training and briefing and has an unmatched reputation for helping individuals, partners and their families to prepare to live and work effectively anywhere in the world.

Through its unrivalled faculty of trainers and experts, Farnham Castle offers a totally flexible and comprehensive range of programmes providing the first-hand knowledge and skills required to be successful in international business including:

- Workshops on developing Cross Cultural Awareness
- Working effectively with specific cultures or nationalities
- Cross Cultural Communication, Presentation and Negotiation skills training
- Country and Business Briefings for any country in the world
- Intensive Tuition in any language

Full details available on web site at:
www.farnhamcastle.com

Introduction

OUR OBJECTIVE

The goal of this book is simple: to help you to be more successful in working with Americans. Whether Americans are your customers, suppliers, colleagues, bosses, or members of your team, the opinions, information, and guidelines offered here are designed to ensure that those relationships are positive and profitable.

This book is addressed to non-American readers who have business contacts in some form with people from the United States. If you plan to be living in American for an extended period, you will find that the full range of topics we cover here will facilitate your adjustment to business life in America. Those of you who are on shorter-term assignments, or who will be frequent business visitors to the States may have particular need for information on establishing relationships, management and teamwork, communication and negotiation styles, and business etiquette and "workplace correctness."

Alternatively, you may be primarily based in your home country, without the need for travel to the States, with responsibilities that involve frequent communication by e-mail or telephone with American partners, colleagues or management. You may also be the "host" to Americans assigned to work in your country. In that case, understanding the "American ways" of management, teamwork and communication is essential.

OUR APPROACH

Our approach is based on helping you develop a practical understanding, not of American "culture" as a whole, but rather of what we have chosen to call the "American way" of business.

Every cultural group views the world in a particular way that is understood by and makes sense to its members. This shared understanding enables them to identify with each other and to deal with the problems of human existence. Americans in particular have evolved certain values, assumptions, and expectations concerning one of those problems – the purpose and conduct of business activities. The interaction of these beliefs, expectations of self and others, and norms of appropriate behavior – call it "business culture" if you like – influences how Americans act and, equally importantly, *how they react to you, the non-American* of a different background.

Much of what you may have already observed or experienced concerning Americans in business may not surprise you. Some of it may even have much in common with business and social behavior in your country. Other aspects, however, may be unexpected, confusing, and even frustrating. We will not be able to cope with those reactions unless we can begin to see the world from their perspective. Our practical understanding starts, therefore, with learning how Americans see themselves, the world as a whole, and the world of business.

When it comes to the various specific aspects of the American way of business, we concentrate on those that often present the greatest challenges to non-Americans. These are covered in detail in Chapters 4 to 8 and concern relationships, motivation, management and teamwork, communication, and negotiation. The questions we pose and the problems we analyze in those areas are based on the actual collected and collective experience of international business people from many countries. They are not based on the theories or research methods of anthropologists, cross-cultural researchers, or social psychologists. These specialists have made some useful observations for us to draw upon, but none of them has ever had to make a presentation to American venture capitalists, take over the leadership of an American company, interview an American job-seeker, or negotiate a service contract with an American customer. Those are the situations where, as we Americans say (borrowing an advertising slogan from the tire industry), "the rubber meets the road" – where the abilities of people are put to the test.

In your dealings with Americans, perhaps you are worried about offending or "turning off" Americans, and want to avoid the "worst case scenarios". Or maybe you prefer instead to focus on making the most of the opportunities that working with Americans offers. Either way, we offer practical strategies for preventing problems, making the right impression, getting results.

NEVER SAY "NEVER"

This is, however, neither a cookbook nor a rulebook. In situations where there are clear "do's and don'ts", for American social and business customs, we point these out. But your individual situation and your experience with Americans will be unique. Business is conducted by people, not by "cultures", or even by organizations. When it comes to dealing with the attitudes and behavior of people of any country, we must talk in terms of possibilities rather than predictions, of understanding before blaming or criticizing, and of applying judgement rather than a list of rules.

BUILDING BRIDGES

Ten out of the eleven chapters in the book are directed at helping *you* to deal with *them*, the Americans. They offer guidelines on understanding American business culture and how to work effectively in it. But in the final chapter we change perspective. There we invite you, the reader, to consider how you can *help the Americans learn from you*, in terms of what you can bring to them in the way of greater international knowledge and fresh perspectives on doing business together. That is a tough challenge, but look at it the way an American would – the glass is half full, not half empty.[1]

The American Way:
A Case of Culture Shock?

America, thou art half-brother of the world;
With something good and bad of every land.

Phillip James Bailey, "The Surface"

Before we attempt to describe, understand and work with
Americans in business, we have to face three important questions:

- Is there any such thing as a "typical American"?
- Is an American, typical or not, different from, say, a Brazilian,
  an Indian, a Swede or even a Canadian when it comes to
  business?
- If there are differences, do they matter? Are they important?

IS THERE A TYPICAL AMERICAN?

In answering the first question, we can take one thing as certain: any
attempt to provide a single uniform description of the beliefs, values,
and behavior of more than 280,000,000 people is impossible.
American is big and diverse. You may think of it as a "melting pot"
or, more fashionably, as a "mosaic" of people of different races,
regions, national origins, and cultural backgrounds. Either way, this
makes it more difficult to define a single "America" in cultural terms.

The question of stereotyping
Despite that certainty, we must also accept that people everywhere

use general labels to describe other groups of people, in the form of stereotyping. People believe that certain traits or characteristics of these groups are not merely typical, but stereo-typical, a word drawn from the printing craft to describe type that is cast from a mould. In other words, a national or ethnic stereotype implies that all members of that group have been identically "moulded". They are all the same.

We would all like to think that we do not stereotype others, but it is in fact a normal response to differences that we observe. We need to generalize; otherwise we would be unable to cope with millions of isolated cases. The danger comes when our stereotypes become prejudices. We then judge others according to these categories, often negatively.

Perhaps you have a stereotype of Americans. You may have met – or may even work with – a person whom you would refer to as "typically American." Through our discussion of the "American way" of conducting business, you may come to alter your stereotype. On the other hand, you may not change your mind at all. Each one of us can find examples from our own store of experience and impression to confirm our own stereotypical images. Each one of us will probably be able to recall an experience that contradicts any of the general tendencies described in these pages. In either cause, it will be helpful for you to be aware of what your stereotype of Americans may be. We will have more to say about that below.

At the same time, we do not want simply to replace one stereotypical view of Americans with another. We cannot predict the behavior of a group of people, nor can we attribute a single fixed set of "values" to it. For every general observation concerning either common American behavior or attitudes toward some aspect of business life, you will find many exceptions.

Sharpening our focus

We can avoid this difficulty by sharpening our focus. Our objective, after all, is to better understand and deal with the Americans you are likely to find *in business*. These people are likely to be fairly well educated by American standards, and in professional or managerial positions – what we in America refer to as "white collar." They may be independent business people, small company entrepreneurs, or members of large multi-national organizations. There will be exceptions here as well, and it would be a mistake to assume that the factory worker, farmer, or supermarket checkout clerk is somehow a different type of American from the rest.

With this narrower focus, we will be better able to make more valid generalizations about Americans, in order to prepare you for possible differences and alternative ways of dealing with them.

ARE AMERICANS TRULY DIFFERENT FROM OTHERS WHEN IT COMES TO BUSINESS?

Here again we can start with a certainty: Americans, like any group, are both similar and different in certain respects to other groups of people. Americans have developed particular ways of answering the universal questions of human society – how to organize and educate themselves, communicate among themselves, and establish relationships of authority and friendship, among others. Their responses are similar in some respects to those of people in other parts of the world, while being different in other ways that reflect the unique conditions and demands of American life. Narrowing our focus to the world of business narrows the range of potential difference. While business people from around the world do many of the same things – negotiate contracts, manage production, organize companies, and so on – most of us would agree that people do not necessarily do these things in the same way.

But where do the differences lie?

Despite the attempts of social scientists to specify and measure these differences objectively through surveys and interviews, what is different depends on one's point of view. How are Americans different from people, or business people, in your country? If you happen to be Japanese, you may look at Americans and see differences in management practices and behavior toward their bosses (they often disagree openly with them). You may also see many similarities between Americans and Europeans. On the other hand, if you come from northern Europe, you may be aware of differences that are less apparent to a Japanese, in certain aspects of communication style, for example. You, too, may see differences in the way Americans relate to their bosses, except that from your perspective they do not disagree with them often enough!

A Venezuelan looks at North Americans and sees a people who have a different approach to social relations and to relations between men and women. If you are Nigerian, you may see a wide range of differences between the people of a developed capitalist society, and those of a developing society with an entirely different heritage.

Before going on to the third of our critical questions, it would be useful for you to think more precisely about your own point of view.

What are your perceptions of Americans?

Using the questions in Box 2.1, make a short list of some of the characteristics of Americans in business that you have observed, based on your experience. Some of these may reflect your stereotype, or image, of the "typical American" in business. They may also reflect the ways in which the Americans whom you have met have been *different* from what you expected.

If you have not yet had contact with Americans, think about what you have heard from others, or the impressions you have formed from books or films.

Box 2.1

Your perceptions of Americans in business

A Based on your experience and impressions of Americans, what characteristics have you observed that make them easy to work with, or may enable you to feel comfortable working with them?

B What characteristics or traits of Americans, in your view, may make them difficult to work with, or present the possibility of conflict or misunderstanding?

Being aware of your own perceptions is a necessary starting point for gaining a greater understanding of the American way of business. We notice these characteristics of other people because we believe that they are evidence of differences between them and ourselves. We will have much more to say about these perceptions below, as we face the third of our critical questions: Are these differences important?

DO THESE APPARENT DIFFERENCES MATTER?

In the arena of international business, it is easy to exaggerate the significance of apparent group-level differences. After all, if we were in reality so very different from each other, we would not be able to do business at all. We would be unable to reach commercial agreements, unable to co-operate, unable ultimately to trust each other. Yet somehow people of different backgrounds have managed to do this, not just in the recent past, but for centuries.

Organizational and environmental factors

We must be careful not to overrate the impact of the "culture" of a nation, group, or society. Many of the differences that you have experienced, or will experience, in working with Americans are due to the requirements and norms of the organisations to which they belong, and business environment in which they operate. As President Calvin Coolidge declared in 1925, "The business of America is business". The day-to-day behavior of people and organisations in America is "driven" (a fashionable American business term for "influenced" or "governed") by a number of practical day-to-day factors:

◆ **The marketplace**
   How competitive is it? In the USA you can normally expect it to be very competitive.

How segmented and differentiated is it? Foreign businesses dream of a share of what appears to be a "single market" of over 280,000,000 people. There is nothing uniform about it, however. In America, market segmentation, according to any demographic or geographic variable you can name, is an art.

In responding to the market, how important is innovation? Marketing? Customer service? Quality? Short development cycles and time-to-market?

◆ **The customers**
Who are they? What do they demand? If the government or public sector is an important customer, adherence to set procedures and standards may be more important than cost control or innovation. Priorities are likely to be different if customers are private sector enterprises.

◆ **Accountability**
To whom does management of the company feel accountable? In most cases this will be shareholders, customers, the financial sector, and the media. Other bodies to whom management may feel accountable include the general public and government regulatory agencies. People from other countries may have an image of American business as being totally free-wheeling law-of-the-jungle capitalism. The reality can be very different. In some sectors, businesses are tightly regulated by federal, state, or local authorities.

◆ **The values of the founder, the chairman, or the chief executive**
America has always offered opportunities to individual entrepreneurs. Their personal leadership or "vision" is often

reflected in the type of people they have selected for their "team", and in the "mission" of the company. We shall have more to say about this aspect of American business life in Chapter 6.

Our list of organizational factors is not necessarily exhaustive. We mention them here to remind you that in preparing to work with Americans, there is no substitute for this knowledge. Indeed, Americans will expect you to come prepared with it.

Despite the diversity of peoples and organizations in America, there is much in the way of outlook, attitudes and behavior that we Americans share, especially when it comes to business. This brings up back to the question of specifying these common elements, and our need to make "informed generalities" about Americans. Let's look again at your general observations in Box. 2.1.

What can you learn from your perceptions of Americans? You can learn at least one thing: differences are important if you believe them to be.

The positive and negative impressions that you listed are clear indications of, on the one hand, areas of likely comfort and compatibility with Americans, and on the other, of potential frustration, misunderstanding, and conflict. We can reduce the potential for frustration by remembering one other thing: those American attitudes and behaviors that appear so confusing, while they may not make sense to you, do make sense to an American, as later chapters will explain.

Your impressions – notably the negative ones – are also a clear indication of something else: of what is important *to you,* according to your background and the way business is done where you come from. To explain better what we mean, let us take an example not relating to America, but to Europe. The British consistently describe Germans as lacking a sense of humor. Whether or not this perception is accurate (it is not!), it says more about the British – that displaying a sense of humor is important to *them,* and that Germans appear to be different in this respect – than about Germans.

In summary then, our perceptions are indicators of (1) where important differences may lie between us and other people; and (2) norms of belief and behavior that are important to us. These perceived differences may or may not culturally shock us, but they are clues to potential or actual problems in the conduct of international business.

In your list of negative impressions of Americans, did you include something like "Americans have little knowledge of other countries"; "They pay little attention to the rest of the world"; or "Americans think that their way is always the best"? Perhaps you included words such as "proud" or "nationalistic". When an American says "globalize" does he really mean "Americanize"?

If the answer is yes, then we need to understand how Americans see themselves and the rest of the world.

The American View of the World

Our starting point for understanding these American attitudes is understanding how we Americans see ourselves as a people. This self-perception or self-belief explains much about our attitudes and responses towards foreigners in business and elsewhere.

WHAT IS AN AMERICAN?

For our discussion, an American is a citizen of the United States of America, someone who identifies himself with those who were brought up there or who live there. But the term "American" in fact applies to many other citizens of the "New World": Mexicans, Costa Ricans and Peruvians, for example see themselves as Americans, too. To them, people from the United States (and English-speaking Canada) are *Norteamericanos*, North Americans. People from Europe, Asia or Africa should keep that in mind when dealing with their friends from Spanish- and Portuguese-speaking America.

Thanks largely to the letters of an otherwise little known Italian sailor named Amerigo Vespucci, which reached a French mapmaker of the early 16th century named Martin Waldseemüller, the entire New World was labelled "Amerigo's land" on maps of the era. Latinized and feminized, the name became "America". The founders of the United States incorporated it into the name of the new nation as the United States *of America*, but the English had already long been referring to their New World colonists as "Americans." In this way, the name came to be associated primarily with people in one large country of North America, at least in the eyes of Europeans. (You may hear a person from the United States who is sensitive to the feelings of Central and South Americans refer to himself or herself as a "U-S American".)

Ideals and symbols

Aside from the name, what is the anchor of the US-American's own identity? What gives this large heterogeneous mixture of people not just a single system of government, but a single identity? Two very concrete and specific things: the US Constitution, and the American flag. The foundation of America is a set of ideals, embodied in a written constitution and the system of government thus established. Those who agree to abide by, protect and support it, are Americans. Belief and pride in one's country and in the Constitution are not the same as belief in the inherent goodness of the governmental authority, however. Many Americans distrust central "government", and see its primary role as the safeguard of freedom and rights, rather than as the primary means of solving social problems, or of managing the economy.

The other more symbolic embodiment of American identity is the flag. Our national anthem is a hymn to it. Our school children "pledge allegiance to the flag of the United States of America, and to the republic for which it stands...". Burning or vandalising it is a crime, and there exists a number of rules pertaining to its display, storage, handling and disposal. Americans, as foreigners often observe, are real "flag-wavers" – and not merely on national holidays, special occasions, or at times of national crisis.

Both the Constitution and the flag in turn represent those ideals of "liberty and justice for all" that define the American identity and focus people's aspirations on the future. American is in a sense a "club" that one chooses to join, or willingly accepts (although African slaves and many native Americans did not originally share in this choice). From these ideals comes a sense of both destiny and mission: America has a responsibility to offer these ideals to all mankind, whether or not other people care to embrace them.

"E pluribus unum" – America as an international country

These unifying factors are strong in America because of, not despite, the heterogeneity of the American people. In addition to seeing its ideals as universal, America sees itself as an "international" country. According to this view, people have come to America from all over the world to become part of this society, and have chosen to leave behind their old ways of life, old ways of thinking, even their families' language and culture to a degree. The Latin motto *E pluribus unum* – "Out of many, one" – which appears on American currency, embodies this belief.

The United States has long been described as nation of immigrants. What many non-Americans may not realize is how true that remains today. According to the census of 2000, the foreign-born population of America was 31.1 million, 11 percent of the total, and a 57 percent increase from 1990. More than half of them are Spanish-speakers. This is the latest of several waves of immigration, of which the heaviest until now occurred during the decade 1900–1910. Many of those immigrants came from southern and eastern Europe, while previous waves brought large numbers from Ireland, Germany and Scandinavia. As early as the beginning of the 18th century, newcomers to "America" from France, Northern Ireland, and the German states, together with earlier settlers from Sweden and Holland, contributed to the formation of a national identity that was already not entirely English.

Attitudes in America toward these succeeding waves of immigrants have always been mixed. New immigrants have sometimes been regarded as threats to public order, to people's jobs, to the public welfare system, to economic stability, or to the established culture or language. The political effect has been a series of measures that have alternated between restriction and permission. But despite these tides of toleration or hostility, immigration has been an essential part of the formation of the United States.

The Americans you are likely to meet in business may not have been part of the latest wave, which has tended to be poor and unskilled. On the other hand, they will very likely have grandparents who were immigrants, and they may still have an attachment to their country of origin, even if it is but a sentimental and romanticized one.

Immigrants brought much more to America than just their languages, religions, and cultures. They brought an attitude. Immigrants, whatever their origin, have been risk takers, seekers of opportunity. They have also been optimists. If you don't think you can make it, you stay home or return home (as many did). As we shall see in later chapters, these same attitudes characterize American businesspeople to this day.

"GLOBALIZING" THE AMERICAN WAY?

At this point, you may be thinking, *"If America is in fact this 'international country', why are Americans often so ignorant of the rest of the world, and unable or unwilling to understand different ways?"*

The answer to that question is a bit of a paradox. The powerful if idealistic example of *"E pluribus unum,"* of unity from diversity, leads many Americans to believe that the American model is universally applicable. "If people from Norway, China, Mexico, Poland, India, Slovakia, Vietnam, and Ethopia can be successful here and live peacefully with their neighbors, why should things be any different elsewhere?" the thinking goes. People are fundamentally similar at the core, and need only a set of rules and a common objective to bring them together. Viewed through American lenses, important differences between people are personal, individual, and circumstantial, rather than collective or cultural.

Race and culture

But what about the question of race in America? Surely that should influence Americans in the direction of a greater understanding of the peoples of the rest of the world.

Despite all the talk of "multi-culturalism", political decisions about race in America are about skin color, not culture. Protected groups of people, for purposes of awarding assistance, providing protection, and granting privilege, are labelled "Asian" or "Hispanic", to give two examples. Yet each of these designations encompasses a multitude of countries and cultures. One prominent American politician claimed a few years ago that America's "management of diversity at home" equipped it to be a leader internationally. This may make some sense to us Americans, but people from South America, Africa, Asia or Europe may not see it the same way. "Managing diversity" inside America has little to do with responding to diversity outside America.

No passport required

An American's knowledge of the rest of the world may also be limited by the size and location of his own country. The United States shares land borders with only two countries: Canada, of which the population, only one-eighth that of the USA, is clustered mainly within 100 miles of the border and Mexico, with a population of over 85 million. This helps explain why only a minority (around 25 percent) of Americans hold passports.

If an American family wishes to take their holidays in the tropics, they need no passport to go to south Florida, Puerto Rico, or the US Virgin Islands. If they prefer somewhere similar to Polynesia, they can go to Hawaii, the 50th state. If for some reason, they are attracted to sub-arctic regions, there is no need to go to Finland, for there is always Alaska. If they want to meet French speaking people, then Quebec is nearer than France, and no passport is needed for Canada. Nor is any required for Puerto Rico, if they want to speak Spanish and enjoy the heritage of Spanish America. Even the area of northern Mexico adjacent to the border is open to US visitors, furnished with only a tourist card.

A belief in the example of their society and the universality of their political and social ideals, often combined with limited experience of "foreign" people, leads Americans to the view that if it works in America, it should work anywhere. If you perceive Americans as not concerned with or knowledgeable about other cultures, ways of life, or value systems, part of the reason lies here.

This in turn has posed certain problems for Americans on an international level, the effect of which you may have experienced. For one, the US-based headquarters of your American parent company may attempt to put in place policies, procedures, and practices for "global" application that take no account of differences elsewhere. For another, the American you meet while on business may have travelled a good deal, but he may lack a true international perspective. The American executive you report to may be so concerned about success in the huge American domestic market, that strategic decisions designed to improve operations in the USA often have the opposite effect internationally.

These problems are due to ignorance, not malice, and so are amenable to solution through education and experience. Other American attitudes are more deeply rooted, and give America much of its strength.

THE AMERICAN WAY OF THINKING – FAITH AND FREE WILL

Two other factors, contradictory in nature, have helped to influence the American mentality: religious faith and the notion of free will, both of which were first brought by the European settlers and immigrants.

From the early Baptist, Puritan, and Quaker settlers who came before them, Americans – whatever their particular personal belief systems, and whether they would admit it or not – have brought to everyday public life a sense of "sin", a moralistic view that often sees right or wrong in "black-and-white" terms. Shades of grey, situational factors, or practical compromises are not the ideal basis for judgments. A compromise may, of course, be the result of a dispute, but many Americans find that a less than satisfactory outcome. One observer put it in even stronger terms – to an American, compromise is "ethically fatal".[1]

Armed with this faith, these early Protestant Christian settlers also brought with them the belief that all people were equal in the sight of God. Through succeeding generations, this belief may have lost something of its explicitly religious association, but none of its force. Truth therefore was not a matter of philosophy, but of religion – it is what you believed. Knowledge, on the other hand, was pragmatic; it grew out of experience.

A further word about religion in America is in order here. Its influence is not simply a matter of spiritual or ethical heritage. Americans, by comparison to other developed nations, are active worshippers. As a visitor or new foreign resident, you may be struck by both the number and variety of places of worship, and the number of people attending. Non-Americans may associate active religious practice in America only with certain sects, or with people of certain political views, but it transcends social classes and political parties. Church attendance and membership meet certain needs in American society, above and beyond that of religious expression. Churches serve as community centers for immigrant and minority groups. They also provide a means of affiliation and belonging, which Americans eagerly seek, and which we discuss at greater length in Chapter 4.

YOURSELF IS ALL YOU'VE GOT

Whatever their particular beliefs, or their degree of intensity, Americans believe that their lives are primarily governed, not by the will of God, but by themselves. In the words of the poet Walt Whitman, "...nothing, not God, is greater to one than one's-self is."[2]

Americans have had comparatively weak attachments to what anthropologists call primary groups: family, native land, social class. Those were left behind by immigrants, and further loosened in the new land by space, mobility, and individual opportunity. The American life is an individual one, defined by the free choices that are the individual's responsibility and under his control. We Americans are constantly exhorted to "be what you want to be", to "be all you can be", or to "take control". Americans approach their business careers with this idea and this drive – realize your ambitions, control your career. There is no such thing as "fate", or "bad luck". If something goes wrong for us, we do not simply accept this as the will of God. Either we show determination and start again, or we find someone to blame. The reality, of course, is that this total control is an illusion, but the belief (or better yet, the faith) in it is a powerful motivator.

Pragmatism and individualism

For an American in business, these influences, while strong, are not the primary immediate basis for daily action. In that respect, American business people are realists, or to put it more precisely, pragmatists. Americans judge the rightness or 'wrongness' of their decisions by one fundamental criterion: *Does it work?* Abstract definitions, theoretical descriptions of validity, philosophical debates on right and wrong – these to an American are pointless. The only thing that matters is: *Does it do the job? Does it meet the need?* That is the very practical point of view of the settler trying to survive in a hostile new land, of the inventor testing an innovation, of the entrepreneur launching a new product.

We can describe that pragmatism even more precisely: "Does it work *for me?*" More than just individuality of thought or individual equality in the sight of God, American individuality is one of individual choice, achievement and action.

The well-known American individualism, which another former President, Herbert Hoover, described as "rugged", originates in 17th century European thought, greatly reinforced by the experience of early settlers. The first English colonists in Virginia and Massachusetts learned the value of individualism the hard way. They at first tried collective economic organization in their communities. Unfortunately for them, that turned out to be ineffective in meeting their most important need – survival. They found that individual ownership, responsibility and reward, in a framework of co-operation under the rules (laws), were the better means to the common good.

While the requirements of building a new society on a new continent demanded individualism, the opportunities available in the new country rewarded it. There was land and wealth enough for everyone, with notable exceptions being the African slaves and the native tribes. Anyone who wanted to work hard could succeed. Individual initiative and effort would bring individual reward. That belief – not unique to the USA, but strongly held there – still characterises the attitudes of Americans in business. The reward – in this world – took the form of wealth. An individual earned this not only by working hard, but also by taking great risks. Failure was viewed as merely a temporary setback. There would always be a chance, an opportunity to start again. Even today, personal bankruptcy or business failure is not a permanent stain on a person's record, a permanent check to one's ambitions. It is no more than a stumble on the road to success.

"Rugged individualism" is a popular phrase, but as we noted above, we Americans are not usually philosophers. We do not enjoy spending our time talking about pragmatism and individualism. We nevertheless feel the influence of these values through our families and our education system.

FAMILY AND SCHOOL

The Americans you are likely to meet have been socialized in a family and school framework that encourages and promotes several important values, which they bring to business:

◆ **Psychological independence** – a reliance on one's own self rather than on the group.

◆ **Co-operation** with other members of a group.

◆ **Financial independence**, or a certain amount of it, often beginning with summer jobs at the age of 16.

- **Personal competitiveness** – personal accomplishment and the desirability of talking about those accomplishments.

- Compared to educational systems in many other countries, **a lack of specialization** until later stages of education.

Growing up American

American middle- and upper-class families are not large. Furthermore, the demands of family obligation – to support, feed, and shelter one another – do not extend much further than the "immediate" family (parents and children). Have you been surprised to see how common it is for older Americans to be housed in "retirement homes", rather than live with their adult children? If this seems harsh to you, it is not viewed the same way by Americans. While it is true that some American adults find their elderly parents a burden rather than a necessary duty, most see this as fully compatible with family love and care. Indeed, in many cases, elderly Americans prefer to live in such communities. In this way, they are in turn freed from the sense that they are a burden to their children. They retain a degree of independence while being able to associate with people like themselves.

The focus on independence and individual achievement starts at a much earlier stage. As a child, my elementary school (roughly ages 8–11, grades 4 through 6) sent "report cards" to my parents on which my "self-reliance" was assessed. This was the degree to which I looked after myself, solved problems on my own, and showed "initiative", the quality whereby a person originates an action or idea. At home, moreover, many American parents now attach a great deal of importance to building their children's self-esteem, rather than their self-discipline. They remind their children daily of how special they are. They praise them frequently and urge them to believe in themselves so that they can "win".

The long summer vacations, normally ten weeks or more, combined with parents' short work vacations of two to three weeks a year mean that families have relatively little extended time to spend together. Summer camps and summer schools fill the gap, giving young Americans time away from their families. By the time they enter university, or even while in high school, most American youth will also have acquired that indispensable tool of freedom, independence, and (hopefully) individual responsibility: the car!

From the age of 16, young people are permitted to find employment in most if not all states. These may be low level manual or service jobs, such as painting houses or waiting on tables in restaurants, but they provide the young American with some financial independence. Most importantly, they also provide an early introduction to the world of work. When it comes time to apply for admission to university, usually at age 17 or 18, the young American can expect that admission officials will want to check that the candidate has spent his summers in a constructive way in some form of employment, study, or volunteer work.

"Bright college years"

Progress through the American educational system and admission to university is far less dependent than in many other countries on the results of competitive examinations. While students are assessed on basic skills and aptitude at various points in their elementary and secondary years, this is only one factor in university admissions. Course work, academic grades, and useful activities outside the classroom are also weighed in the balance. The last factor is very important. It may include previous employment or volunteer work, as already mentioned. It may also include membership and leadership responsibilities in school clubs or student organizations. You can see how at a young age, the profile of the "active doer" so admired by employers – independent, achieving, co-operative, and responsible – is being formed.

However strong his or her profile, an American student has to "sell" himself in the competitive arena of university admissions. This is done partly by letters and essays that may support an application. It is also done, crucially, in the admissions interview. Here, the candidate must talk about his accomplishments, appear to have clear goals and objectives (however vague and tentative in reality), and give specific reasons (even if somewhat hypocritical) for wanting to attend a specific college or university. These same skills will help that student to find employment after graduation, and to advance his career subsequently.

So what do Americans learn from their education, and how?

The first response we can offer is – not enough, according to both American and foreign observers. Standardized international comparisons of scholastic achievement find American students ranked well down in the table, especially in mathematics. As you have probably found, few if any will learn a foreign language to a competent level, if at all.

At the four-year college or undergraduate level, leading to the BA or BS, American students will have an opportunity to pursue a speciality (known as a *major*) while retaining considerable flexibility, in the event they change their minds as to field or eventual career. The undergraduate's preparation for graduate studies in law, medicine, or engineering will involve a greater concentration on relevant subjects. There are also increasingly specialised Bachelor degrees in fields ranging from media to information technology. In 2001, degrees in business accounted for 21 percent of the total. But the field in which a graduate has earned his Bachelor's degree does not necessarily predetermine his choice of career or graduate study. This is especially true in the case of the MBA (Master's Degree in Business Administration).

As far as methods are concerned, American educational methods do not emphasize comprehensive mastery or rote learning of a body of literature, information, or texts. This is very different from cultures such as the Arab or the Chinese, where intensive scholarship is demanded and respected. American schools prefer instead to emphasize "self-expression" in various forms – creativity, individual points of view in analysis and opinion, novelty.

Americans usually finish their undergraduate education at age 22. (There has been a recent trend toward later completion, possibly as a result of the expense of a college education.) At this point, if they are not going directly on to graduate school, American graduates are ready, although certainly not yet "seasoned", for employment in business. They hope that there will be no more painting houses, or waiting on tables.

Class ring

In our discussion of the objectives and content of American
education, we must not overlook one other benefit that the
undergraduate experience brings to an American – friends.

Most American university students live in residence halls
(dormitories) on campus for four years. It is rare to live at home
or in rented rooms. Students may also join, if invited, more
intimate groups, called *fraternities* or *sororities*. Residing together
on campus enables Americans to establish close ties with each
other, something that will be far more difficult after they leave. It
gives them a vital sense of group membership and belonging. It is
here that they may well make friends and form a network, often
for life. Many Americans wear a "class ring", on which is
engraved both the name of the college or university and the year
("class") in which they took their degree. This identity badge can
serve later in life as a link to a strong network of fellow former
students (or *alumni/alumnae*), or at the very least as a reason to
get better acquainted with ones they meet.

But if, as a foreign visitor to the United States, you have no
"class ring", how will you establish strong relationships and
lasting friendships with Americans? In your list of perceived
American characteristics, did you include "friendly"?
"Superficial"? Both? Let us turn our attention now to this aspect
of American life. The success of your business relationships and
the satisfaction you derive from your expatriate life in the USA
will depend on it.

Getting to Know You: Social and Business Relationships

"EASY COME..." – GETTING ACQUAINTED WITH AMERICANS

Have you ever experienced something similar to this incident?

EXAMPLE 4.1

Imagine for a moment that you have just settled into your aisle seat on a long-distance flight to Chicago. A moment later, another passenger arrives, and indicates that he has the seat next to yours. As you stand to permit him to get through, he says "Excuse me, looks like the flight is full..." and starts to comment on how airlines never manage the boarding process smoothly.

He takes his seat, and continues to chat to you. He says his name is Charlie, and he's returning to Dayton Ohio after calling on European customers to sell telecommunications equipment. He goes on to explain that he's been away for three weeks, and misses his wife and kids. He doesn't think his eldest daughter has missed him very much, however, since she's trying to show how "cool" and independent she is. Charlie expresses worry about his son, Justin, who's having trouble in school.

He asks you, "Do you have kids?"

The airplane begins to pull away from the departure gate...

◆ What's your reaction to this?

- I will enjoy passing the time on this flight talking to this friendly man.

- I will listen politely, but will not feel like talking about my life so soon in the same way.

- Charlie is inconsiderate and annoying; on this long flight in this crowded cabin, it would be more polite if he kept to himself.

Or this?

EXAMPLE 4.2

On a visit to the States, you and some American business colleagues have just taken your seats at a restaurant table. A waitress approaches and starts by saying, "Hi, my name is Michelle and I'll be your server today."

One of your American colleagues replies, "Hi, Michelle. Can you give us a couple of minutes and then we'll be ready to order?"

What is going on here?

- Michelle wants to get to know us better while she serves our table, so we should tell her our names.

- Michelle wants a large tip when the bill (the "check" in America) arrives, and is being friendly only for that reason.

- You have entered a "gentlemen's club" by mistake.

- Michelle is acting toward you in the same way that she would toward any customer.

Exaggerations? Caricatures of Americans? Possibly, but many non-Americans have had similar encounters, and are confused by such behaviour. Did you answer **(b)** or **(c)** in the first example? Perhaps you perceive Americans as "friendly," or "superficial". This immediate friendliness and informality can make people uncomfortable, precisely because it seems insincere. This is a reflection of the manner in which social and business friendships are formed in America and the meaning of these friendships, which may be very different from what is expected in your country.

A degree of "superficial" friendliness is important to us Americans. Rapid and friendly social interactions are normal. In a large country where people move around frequently, contact of this type is both essential and unavoidable. Friendliness conveys to an American the right degree of both social distance (or closeness, if you prefer) and social acceptance. An American takes this to mean, "I like you."

"But what's the point", you may ask, "of talking about your son's problems at school with a complete stranger, if you then go your separate ways and, in that big country, never see each other again?"

Not every conversation at first meeting will include such personal details, but it is not unusual. With those disclosures, an American seeks to establish a commonality of experience with a stranger, while affirming his own social identity. This is preferable to an abstract discussion of world affairs, the arts or other impersonal matters, with which you might be more comfortable. To an

American, Charlie is in fact being polite. It would be impolite, "stand-offish", or even rude *not* to initiate some contact with you, a fellow passenger. To ignore you would be to take no notice of you – to reject you, in a sense – as a human being. We Americans may like our wide open spaces, but we do not like isolation.

Call me "Jim"

The immediate use of first names is expected, once any necessary titles have been mentioned. We will have more to say about titles and greetings below. For our server (a description preferable to "waitress") Michelle, *not* mentioning her name would be impersonal, and referring to herself as "Ms" or "Mrs Ames" would be unnecessarily formal. One's last name (not "surname") is unimportant when it comes to getting to know people. This is another contemporary habit that has its roots in the social development of American society. When settlers from Europe established a new society in the New World, their last names no longer served as indicators of occupation, origin, social class, or rank in the same way as they did in Europe. Last names were retained as "family names". In a social context, the use of first names signalled equality of status, and served as an indicator of direct personal contact.

Perhaps you come from a culture in which people prefer a greater degree of social distance when getting acquainted, by using titles more frequently, or by different ways of addressing "you" (*Tu* or *Usted* in Spanish, *Du* or *Sie* in German). If so, American informality may seem like a case of "too close too fast".

When it comes to establishing social and business relationships with Americans, two points are worth remembering here:

♦ If you wait too long before entering into this American informality, you may appear to us Americans as reserved, too formal, or (a word we used previously) stand-offish. To an American businessperson, that implies that you may not really be interested in doing business.

♦ On the other hand, do not be misled by an American's apparent closeness or intimacy. To illustrate, let's "fast-forward" our in-flight scenario to the moment when you touch down at the airport in Chicago.

"...EASY GO" – FRIENDLINESS WITHOUT FRIENDSHIP

American girl, she tell a lie –
She say, " 'Til then,"
She mean, "Goodbye."

Chuck Berry, "Havana Moon"

EXAMPLE 4.3

Let's imagine for a moment that as your plane comes to its arrival stand in Chicago, Charlie says, as he is retrieving his property from the overhead compartment, "I really enjoyed meeting you, ———— (*Insert your name here*). Here's my card. If you're ever in Dayton, give me a call and we can get together for dinner. My wife would enjoy meeting you, too."

How do you respond?

♦ I would offer him my card, and invite him to my hometown in a similar way. I would not expect either event to happen, however.

◆ Charlie is being completely hypocritical. His invitation is not a real invitation. I would simply say, "Thank you and I hope you make your connecting flight."

◆ He is offering his hospitality, and I should accept the invitation, if at all possible.

Your response will, of course, depend on many factors, especially on whether you enjoyed his company enough to want to continue the acquaintance. (A woman would be less likely to extend this type of "invitation" to a man, for fear it would be misinterpreted.) If your answer was (a), then perhaps you are used to this sort of interaction between strangers on a plane. Charley probably sees the situation in the same way.

"But if he does not expect that your paths will ever again cross, then why does he bother inviting you? Surely this is somehow dishonest."

If that went through your mind, then you may have answered (b). From the American point of view, Charlie's "invitation" is a polite way of expressing his enjoyment at having made your acquaintance, and his wish that you might meet again. It is at the same time an implied regret that the two of you will revert to being strangers. And so you do.

If you answered (c) then you come from a culture that attaches a great deal of importance to the offering and acceptance of hospitality. Americans attach far less importance to this, and you may be disappointed.

"No cost, no obligation"

Our little scenario, which could have a dozen different endings, offers several useful lessons concerning the American way of friendship in a number of situations. Foreign students in America, for example, have often complained that Americans, while very friendly, simply do not form any bonds after a first meeting. There is no follow-up. The foreign student expects a closer relationship – more time together, more sharing – but very little is forthcoming.

It is true that American friendships often involve less obligation and fewer ties than many non-Americans expect. This can be frustrating if, like the students, you are going to live and work in America for an extended time. Lack of good friendships with local people can be a great source of dissatisfaction. The Americans you meet at the office or in the neighborhood may be very warm and welcoming at the beginning. They may offer to help you visit the city, move into your home, or get to know your new colleagues at the office. But later, little more may be offered. And you wonder, "Why not?"

The American friendliness is sincere, but the American expectation of friendship is that it makes few demands, offers no real commitment, and expects very little in return. In this way, Americans retain their independence. They remain free from obligation to others, and from the discomfort of having others obligated to them. Charlie does not expect you to accept his invitation, and will not press it. For his part, once the two of you have gone your separate ways, he may feel little obligation to deliver on his invitation.

Even many longer-term friendships can end comparatively quickly. If people move away to a new place, they start again with new friends. If two friends quarrel, they may simply drift apart, rather than reconcile themselves through confrontation or the mediation of a third person.

Friends at work?

What does "friendship" mean to you? In the society in which you were brought up, friendship may imply a strong obligation to do as much as you can for a friend – lend money, travel a long way to help, offer a place to stay for an indefinite period. A friend doesn't need to ask, doesn't need to say thanks. There is a strong expectation that your friend would do the same for you. Americans do not expect nearly as much. The same is true in the workplace.

EXAMPLE 4.4

An Indian engineer in an electronics company believes that her American colleagues, while friendly, do not trust her. When she asks for information and assistance, they ask very direct questions in return: "Why exactly do you need this, Priya?" "What's this for?" She is annoyed that she has to explain her requests. She does not have the same problem with her Indian colleagues.

Is she right about the Americans?

◆ Yes. Their behavior is a clear indication that they do not trust her, or have confidence in her, perhaps because she is female and Indian.

◆ Yes. Their behavior is a clear indication that they do not trust her, or have confidence in her. She should know that she needs to explain precisely what she wants and why. ▶

♦ No. They are responding in a way that Americans would expect, but both sides may be misinterpreting or overlooking some important signals, such as tone of voice.

Neither **(a)** nor **(b)** is a likely explanation, except under particular circumstances. In this situation, our Indian engineer's relationship with her Indians colleagues may be one in which the bonds of mutual obligation are strong. They would assist Priya with "no questions asked". The Americans, on the other hand, will have a different expectation of this relationship. Someone who asks for something with no explanation is, in effect, acting as if the other person is *obliged* to provide it. This to an American expresses an attitude of superiority.

At work, your friendly American colleagues or co-workers will feel relatively little obligation to support you, to do you favors, to reciprocate when you do them favors, regardless of the warmth of your relationship. Yet we certainly do not mean that Americans *will* not be generous with their support, time, or assistance. We are simply saying that, after the first contact, they may not feel *obliged to be* generous – you need to ask for what you need, and explain why.

This pattern that we've just described is one with hundreds of exceptions. The pattern among women, for example, may be somewhat different to that among men. It may be different within certain particular groups of people. One description of American culture suggests that within the American military, and among African-Americans, the obligations and expectations of friendship are stronger than the norm.[1]

What we have described here is an aspect of the American way of life than can cause some culture shock in newcomers. It may be hard to get accustomed to this strange culture with its smiling faces, friendly greetings, and weak attachments. This will take time, and you cannot expect too much based on the first contact. Lasting friendships will nevertheless develop, provided you work at it.

To make that adjustment easier, let's look at the American way of "socialising".

"LET'S DO LUNCH!" – MEETING AMERICANS AT HOME, OFFICE AND ELSEWHERE

Networking

For Americans in business, the most important reason to meet people is to "network". There is in America both a need and a preference for this form of contact, as it involves no friendship but depends on friendliness. Precisely because they have few strong ties to large families or political groups, Americans have to create their own networks, based on rapid acquaintances made at professional conferences, social events, and – yes – on airplanes.

Networking is certainly not a uniquely American practice, but it is one with which we are very comfortable. We are normally very open about it; some non-Americans might say even a bit "forward". It is taken for granted as a possible outcome when business people, who may otherwise be strangers, happen to start talking together in any setting. We network in order to make sales contacts, obtain information, find a lead to a new job. We are not limited by social rank or status, and networking can quite easily occur between a man and a woman (as long as the conversation focusses on business).

Is Charlie from Dayton on the plane simply networking with you? Is he being friendly simply in order to find out if you can be of some use to him?

That's not likely, given the American need and preference for the kind of social contact described in the previous section. But if your chat took you into areas of mutual business interest, you may become part of his network (and he of yours). This may be signified by an exchange of business cards at the end of your flight, and implies the possibility, though not the certainty, of future contact.

Americans find opportunities to network not only in casual encounters, but also in organized groups. These may include various professional associations, some of which exist largely for that purpose, whatever their stated goals may be. Other organizations have a more obvious and focussed networking character. Chambers of Commerce are an example.

At the same time, community service groups such as Rotary Clubs, Lions Clubs, or Junior League provide their American members with more than a collection of potentially useful "contacts". They offer a deeper sense of purpose, belonging, and group identity. You may be familiar with, or even a member of, one of these organizations. There are many other "fraternal" organisations in America, such as the Elks or the Kiwanis Clubs, that provide a framework for both social and community service activities. In addition, church membership, though based on spiritual needs, may also offer similar benefits. Indeed you may find that in areas of the USA where church membership and attendance is high, members may form loose business networks.

A recommendation: If you are going to be living in America for an extended period, you should look into the possibility of membership in one of these organizations. In some cases, you will need to be nominated or sponsored for membership, so admission may not occur immediately. If you are an international member, then take advantage of your association in the States. You will be welcomed with that quick friendliness that we have described, and will find it a convenient setting for meeting people.

Home and away – where and how to meet Americans

Establishing real friendships with Americans, however, is likely to take some time. We have seen how a non-American should not expect too much from a first meeting, no matter how friendly and warm it may seem.

While living in the USA, there are several alternatives if you wish to improve your chances of meeting Americans with whom you may have something in common:

◆ Look for other kinds of special interest groups, such as local hobby clubs. If you are with your family in America, this could involve them as well (assuming that they tolerate your hobby!). Local charity/volunteer organizations, open to all, are another possibility.

◆ Ask colleagues at work about the organizations to which they may belong. Say that you (and your family) are interested in meeting people. We Americans, great joiners and networkers that we are, will fully empathise, and may offer some useful ideas. We will certainly not think that you are, being "too forward".

◆ If your wife or husband is accompanying you, but is not permitted to work, she or he may choose to attend adult education classes of some kind. These are an excellent setting for making acquaintances with people. Indeed, many Americans participate in these for precisely that purpose.

Getting to know your colleagues

One of your colleagues at work may invite you to an after hours event such as a sporting match (American football, basketball, ice hockey, or baseball). It will probably not be an occasion for extended conversation, but it's a start. So by all means, accept the invitation and expect to pay for your own ticket. Later, assuming that your time together was pleasant enough, it would be appropriate for you to suggest to your colleague, "Let's go out for dinner," and invite him to join you at a restaurant.

You may also invite him or her (although not normally *her* alone), together with spouse/partner, to dinner at your home. If you have children, then make it a two family affair. If you do not have children, and would prefer that they not bring theirs, then make clear to your friend for whom the invitation is intended: "Would *you and Liz* [by not mentioning their kids, you are excluding them] be able to come to dinner at our place?" Americans do less home hospitality than others, and are not as spontaneous when it comes to offering or accepting invitations, so give them plenty of notice: at least a week; ten days to two weeks is better. Remember: Americans do not willingly take on obligations, so your colleague may not feel obliged to accept. Do not be offended if they cannot. In a later section we offer some additional comments on the subjects of invitations and hospitality with business colleagues.

Social etiquette

We are an informal people, with little in the way of ritual or protocol accompanying our getting to know each other. There are, however, several guidelines that can help ensure that you establish the right degree of social contact, without somehow putting Americans off.

When first meeting an American face-to-face, at a business meeting or in a social situation, give your first name followed by your last (not the reverse, as some French or Chinese people might do). It is not necessary to state your title (Mr., Mrs., Dr., etc.), unless it is a very formal occasion. But do not give your last name only (as some Germans might do), unless that is how you wish to be addressed by the Americans. Once you have been introduced, then you can normally use first names only; Americans will expect it. If you continue to use titles and/or last names, it will appear as if you are trying to keep too great a distance.

Titles should be used in the following circumstances:

♦ On the outside and inside address of a letter, and the salutation. ("Dear Dr. Simpson,...")

- ◆ When you are introducing an American with a doctorate (Ph.D.) in a formal setting, such as a speech or presentation. ("Our next speaker is Dr. Andrea Cummings...")

You may then revert to first names after the event, or once you have met or spoken on the telephone.

With American women, the title Ms. (pronounced *miz*), intended to be an equivalent to Mr. without marking marital status, should be used in formal direct address in writing or when first speaking on the telephone. It should also be used with the addressee's last name in letter salutations. ("Dear Ms. Morelli,...") Again, once two-way contact has been established, you then can normally use her first name.

There is no need to use Mrs. or Miss in these situations, unless these are specifically indicated on a woman's business card or other correspondence from her.

Americans of both sexes will normally indicate their professional and academic titles on their business cards, but not their social titles (Mr., Ms., etc.).

Greeting people

EXAMPLE 4.5

A Russian who had just started work in an American company encountered an American colleague in the office hallway, who asked him, "Hi, Yuri, How are ya doing?"

Yuri began to answer with information on the new house he had just bought, and the problems that he had finding his way around the office. He was surprised to see his colleague continuing to walk away from his down the hall!

"If you don't care about the answer to your question, then why did you ask me?" thought Yuri.

It is polite in America to always greet someone you know (or in the case of Charlie, even someone you don't know). This is generally true if it involves a colleague at work whom you pass frequently in the office corridors, even if you have spoken to this person shortly before. A quick acknowledgement in passing ("Hi, Pam...") is enough.

Americans will do the same to you, but they do not expect to stop and chat, even if they say, "How are you?" or "How ya doin'?" These are not normally intended as conversation starters, but are simply greetings. If any reply is in order, "Fine, thanks," is suitable.

If you are with a friend, family member, or colleague and happen to meet an American whom you know in the supermarket, at work, or elsewhere, you should *always* introduce them to each other. It would be rude not to. The Americans will do the same to you, if they meet someone they know while you are accompanying them. Again, status, rank, relationship, or whether you had previously been properly introduced mean nothing.

Invitations
When an American invites you to lunch, dinner or an outing of

some kind, you should accept or decline quickly and clearly. In America, it is not expected that you would hesitate or hold back, thinking that the other person will press the invitation further. Perhaps you come from a country where this is more common, and considered polite. In America it will be taken at face value, as "No, thank you." Your American friend is likely to say simply, "Maybe another time, then." In so doing, he is not indicating that the invitation was insincere, but is simply respecting your independence, without any further obligation on either side. So if you wish to accept, say so. If you wish to decline, a simple expression of regret that you cannot for such-and-such a reason is sufficient. No offense will be taken. Let him propose another time if he so desires.

For formal dinners, a written invitation would always be sent, normally with the notation R.S.V.P. This is an abbreviation of the French phrase *Répondez s'il vous plaît*. ("Please reply".) You should therefore send back a reply.

As Americans are generally very punctual, you should plan to arrive at the time stated in the invitation with a delay of no more than 15 minutes. Phone ahead to let them know if you are going to be much later than that. Under no circumstances should you arrive early, unless you have been asked to help in the kitchen! If you are invited to dinner with a small group (two or three other couples, for example) at a restaurant or someone's home, even tighter (although not exact) punctuality is expected.

An "open house" is altogether different. If you come from a part of the world where this is a common form of hospitality, you know the routine. This event will take place over a stated time interval, for example, from 7:00 p.m. to 9:30 p.m., or perhaps on a weekend afternoon. Guests can arrive at any point during that time, and then serve themselves. There is no need to bring anything. For a "pot luck", on the other hand, every guest brings a dish that they have prepared. Usually the host or hostess will let you know what sort of dish is needed: "vegetable", "main dish", "dessert" or something else.

Meeting Americans in their homes

When invited to dinner at the home of an American business associate or colleague, it is polite to ask the host or hostess if you can "bring something" and then take their cue as to whether wine, chocolates, or some other delicacy would be appropriate. If they reply that there is no need to bring anything, you should still bring a moderately priced bottle of wine or, if that is not appropriate for you, flowers. Your hosts will not be offended if you do not bring anything, but they may be mildly surprised. A small item or gift from your country is another possibility, but this should not be of great value. Americans are not accustomed to giving gifts on these occasions.

The evening will proceed according to the European manner, with some important American variations. Guests will normally first be offered drinks, followed fairly shortly thereafter by the meal. They will remain to continue conversations after the meal is finished. It is not expected that men and women will form separate groups at that point. That might occur, based simply on areas of common conversational interest, but normally men and women will participate together in the general conversation.

It would be rare if your hosts were smokers, so do not expect that people will smoke. If you must, ask if you can do so "outside". The best policy, when visiting most American homes, is to forget about it, *even for outdoor gatherings.*

So what should you be prepared to talk about? What subjects should you avoid?

"Small talk"

In the world of international business, people from different countries find that they have a number of subjects that provide ample opportunity for "small talk": the weather, traffic, air or train travel, the cost of living (and in the USA, the cost of a house!), to name a few. Americans may, however, feel comfortable making conversation on topics which may embarrass you. For example, when an American expresses admiration for an object in your home, and asks where you acquired it, this does not indicate that he desires it. The American would be surprised and embarrassed if you then offered it to him!

Conversely, if you find yourself in an American's home, your host may be quite happy to tell you how much he paid for a lamp, a painting, or the home cinema system, and "what a great deal" it was. It would be somewhat rude of an American to do this if you had not first expressed admiration for the object in question, but it happens. (You need not act similarly toward American guests!)

Be prepared for the fact that much conversation will still be about business. This is for a couple reasons. First, it is an activity that you have in common, a "shared experience" if you like, and a very important one to Americans. They do not mind discussing business anytime, anywhere. Secondly, they may not be ready to talk with you about American politics, or about conditions in your country, on which they may not be well informed. Your American friends will not usually try to hide any lack of knowledge; they may display much curiosity and ask many questions about your home country.

Talking politics

As far as politics is concerned, you may find that your American hosts or guests express fairly cautious views at first, since a political discussion is not many Americans' idea of a good way of getting to know you. Friendliness is the most important aspect of such a gathering. They may well hold strong positions on the political and social questions in the USA, but are not likely to want to reveal them at the early stages of your relationship.

For your part, you may wish to get their reaction to certain critical comments that you or others have made about America. Just remember that as an outsider – and this is just as true in other parts of the world – you have only a limited "right" to criticize your host country. For the most part, Americans are largely supportive of their system of government and, as many people have observed, proud of their country, even though they may strongly disagree with the policies of their national, state, or local authorities. It would be appropriate to ask about an American election campaign or about the system or local government where you are. This focuses the political conversation on a more impersonal footing, with which Americans may be more comfortable.

Religion

It is also not advisable to inquire as to your friends' religion. If the conversation happens to turn to that topic, then you are on safer ground in discussing it. But in all these sensitive subjects, take your cue from your American friends.

Race

Race is another very sensitive topic. Americans are not accustomed to discussing this question on social occasions, and fear embarrassing themselves or their listeners by saying something insensitive or unfashionable. The relative openness with which people from other racially mixed societies such as South Africa or Malaysia talk about race is rare in the USA.

And afterward?

What happens the next day? Perhaps not as much as you expect. Your American hosts will be pleased to receive a thank-you note, but will not be offended if you do not send one. Nor will they expect a reciprocal invitation from you. Again, no obligations are involved. As a host, the converse applies. You may or may not receive a thank-you note (or e-mail, or phone call) from your American guests. To them, a warm "thank you" when leaving your home at the end of the evening is enough. You may or may not receive an invitation to their home in similarly intimate circumstances. Whatever happens, you are part of their circle of friends now. Your return invitation may be weeks or even months later, perhaps to a picnic or barbecue, with a number of other people.

When we pointed out in Chapter 2 the difficulty of predicting Americans' behavior, this is area is a case in point. You will experience variations on the practices described here, but these general observations are a reliable basis for noting those exceptions.

WORK OR PLAY? – BUSINESS HOSPITALITY WITH AMERICANS

While your social contacts and friendships will develop through your visits to American homes, many of your business relationships, especially if you are a visitor, will develop through time spent in restaurants, bars, golf courses and other such places. A few guidelines concerning commonly expected behavior and etiquette may be useful here.

Business lunches and drinks

If you are a supplier calling upon a prospective customer for the first time, the customer will prefer, and indeed expect, that this first contact will take place in their office, rather than at a restaurant, bar, or café.

Later on, as your relationship progresses to business lunches, it is commonly expected that the supplier will pay. If the customer or prospective customer has a strict policy against this, as is often the case, then each person pays his own share. (This is referred to informally as "Dutch treat" or "going Dutch", an old English expression originating in stereotyped descriptions of people from Holland as being thrifty to the point of being ungenerous.) In this way, each person avoids the obligation to reciprocate, and keeps his independence. Therefore you should show courtesy to an American who invites you out to lunch, a drink, or dinner by offering to pay for what you consume.

Apart from paying for his own share, your American friend will not expect lunch to be lengthy. He will also expect that the conversation will balance "small talk" with business matters. Avoiding business altogether may cause an American to feel like he is wasting that most precious resource – time.

Hospitality toward colleagues

Are you the leader of a team of Americans? If so, and want to offer hospitality to your colleagues at your new home in America, it is best to do this with the whole group together, rather than one by one. This sort of gathering is somewhat less common practice in the USA than in other countries, Britain for example. Americans will probably be more comfortable initially with an informal gathering, such as a picnic or barbecue. This is also more practical and easier to prepare than a dinner at home. But if the weather does not allow this kind of "get-together", there is no hurry; you can wait until it does.

Remember: The good atmosphere of your hospitality, at home or in a restaurant, may be strained by three factors. The first is the increasing lack of tolerance on the part of many Americans for people who smoke. Secondly, Americans may drink little, for various reasons – health, driving, not wanting to embarrass themselves. Third, Americans may not be willing to "let their hair down" and talk freely or jokingly in the presence of you or colleagues. They risk "offending" someone present, and the fact of being in a public restaurant or at someone's home does not exempt the company from possible responsibility for such "offensive" behavior. See Chapter 9 for more on this.

Smaller, more informal and entrepreneurial organizations are likely to view these matters in a correspondingly more relaxed way. But again, do not expect Americans to behave in the same way as people in your country might in the same setting.

Finally, we should note here that Americans do relatively little after-work drinking with colleagues. If you come from Japan or Britain, you may feel a bit lonely after the end of the working day! Things may be different when there is a special occasion, such as a birthday. Otherwise, Americans may prefer going to the gym, to their evening activities, or home to their families.

Behind the smile

We noted earlier that international business is conducted by people, not by "cultures". When people meet, it is their unique personalities and purposes that determine the outcome, so each encounter will be unique. But if your perceptions of Americans include such attributes as "open", "superficial", "friendly", "insincere", perhaps it is easier now to see what lies behind the smile.

Unlike people in many other parts of the world, such as Asia and South America, Americans want to get to know you, not *before* doing business but *by* doing business. Friendliness helps make this possible, but what matters is what people *do* together. That is the measure of a business relationship, and as we shall see in the next chapter, that is the measure of success.

5

The American at Work: Expectations of Job, Career, and Company

All his life he [the American] jumps into the train after it has started and jumps out before it has stopped; and he never once gets left behind, or breaks a leg.

George Santayana

LIVE TO WORK, OR WORK TO LIVE?

So far we have looked at Americans' concept of their identity as a people and nation, and described their view of society and the rest of the world. We have also described attitudes and expectations that they acquire through family life and education, and highlighted their approach to social relationships. What affect do all these influences have on the way Americans do business?

What is your view? What are your perceptions of Americans' attitude toward work and their jobs? What impressions do you have of their "work ethic"?

Many non-Americans have formed a fairly distinct impression of Americans as a people who "live to work", rather than "work to live". This implies that work is somehow central to life, or indeed an end in itself, as opposed simply to being a means to the end of providing for oneself or one's family. Both perceptions are of course oversimplifications, but the phrase "live to work" contains an important truth about Americans. Many non-Americans perceive that this attitude translates into "hard work", while others see it as expressing itself through "activity without effectiveness" – a great deal of apparent work without much result. Either way, it underlines the centrality of work in the lives of Americans.

We can get an insight into this and other aspects of an American's approach to work and career by looking at one person's resume. (Pronounced *resumé*. The terms *CV* and *curriculum vitae* are not generally used in the USA.)

Study the resume in **Example 5.1**. After you have read it, consider these questions and note your immediate reactions:

◆ What impression do you form of this person?

◆ What do you think this person is trying to communicate about herself?

◆ According to your business background, what information would you want or expect to see on a resume that is *not* presented here?

For our purposes, we can look at this resume in two ways. The first is to take it for what it is – a specific type of document for a specific purpose. In Chapter 9, we will have more to say about the content of the American resume. The second – and the one that concerns us most here – is to see it as the concrete expression of a number of essential American assumptions and expectations

Example 5.1.

LENORE MADISON

1338 Van Dryden Blvd Apt. 12

Kenosha, Wisconsin

tel: (414) 555-8302 fax: (414) 555-8308

e-mail: lmadi@bpm.com

CAREER OBJECTIVE

Position in Product Marketing, utilizing my skills in CRM*, account management, promotion, and public relations.

EXPERIENCE

June 2002 to date: **Marketing Services Manager, Midwest Region.** Schaffer Products, Milwaukee.

◆ Planned and managed new product launch, enabling SP to exceed first quarter sales target by 35%.
◆ Managed design and production of all technical and promotional literature for the region.
◆ Organized customer/professional seminars, improving attendance by 45%.
◆ Designed and successfully installed customer and product database.

December 99 – June 02: **Marketing Support Specialist.** North & Kyle Instruments, Inc. Chicago.

◆ Prepared press releases and marketing brochures for entire range of N&K products.
◆ Maintained customer database of 450 customers, exceeding service level agreement of 95% accuracy.
◆ Designed Proposal format to be used by all N&K salespeople.

January 98 – December 99: **Marketing Assistant.** Co-Therm Products, Hamilton, New Jersey.

◆ Edited and Published internal Sales/Marketing Newsletter.
◆ Scheduled and handled administration for annual Co-Therm Executive Institute, and six other customer events.
◆ Supported all sales campaigns and proposals with accurate and on-time distribution of all required marketing information.

Summer 1996: Intern, Marketing Department, Co-Therm Products.

EDUCATION

MBA (evening program): North Illinois Institute, Schaumberg, Illinois.

BA: English Literature, North Jersey College.

ACTIVITIES

Junior League of Kenosha. Project Leader – Community Literacy Project.

*Customer Relationship Management

concerning the world of work: one's job, the organization, one's career, management and indeed oneself.

Many of these assumptions and expectations are not unique to Americans, but both in their strength and in conjunction with each other, they are particularly characteristic of Americans. What is more, they are developed from an early age, indeed earlier than is the case for most non-Americans.

"I am what I do!"

In your list of perceived attributes of Americans, you may have noted "competitive". If so, you are right. But what is important for us to understand is the nature and basis of this "competitiveness", and what it means for you if you are working with or directing Americans like Ms. Madison.

We have already seen in Chapter 3 that your American business associate has been brought up in a competitive culture. He has learned, as a teenager, to compete for admission to university and for employment. Lenore Madison shows that she understands the means of competition – first and above all, on the basis of your "track record", your accomplishments and achievements. Does her resume seem to you to be simply a list of things she claims to have achieved? If so, you're right again. What is important to an American in business is **accomplishment**, in concrete measurable terms. That is the definition of a person's professional worth and value. That is *who she is*, professionally speaking. Simply put, an American would say, "I am what I do, what I have done, and what I can do."

This is a very egalitarian value. My worth is not matter of my family or class background, although that can give me an advantage. Nor it is a matter of whom I know or where I come from, although those factors too can help. It is not even a matter of how intelligent or knowledgeable I may be. It depends on what I have achieved. In Lenore's case, her list is intended to declare her value, to both future and current employers, in the terms that they most recognise – what we in America (and in business schools everywhere) call **performance.**

Your American colleague, boss, or customer is wholly oriented toward getting things done. This applies if it means getting something done less than perfectly, or even if it means getting something done that someone else has previously done, known as "reinventing the wheel". He or she wants to be known, above all, as a doer, not as a thinker, planner, or even a communicator.

It is also important to *be seen* to be doing things. To fill time with activity is an apparent need among American families as well as among American business people.

"Time is money"

This well-known phrase "says it all" for Americans. Time is something to gain or lose, spend or save, invest or waste. It is also something that one can "make" or "kill"; or it is like an empty vessel that one can "fill", with activity, with doing things. This applies at both work and play. To quote Benjamin Franklin, "Leisure is time for doing something useful..."

If one's professional worth is determined by one's record of achievement, then activity is the appropriate way to use time, preferably short periods of time. American business people focus on and are motivated by short-term objectives. Even if these are not always achievable, they hold the promise of quick accomplishments. Long-term planning, while useful, is far less attractive. This is not because the plan or goal might not be achievable, but because the individual responsible for it may have moved on by the time it is due. He may not be in a position to see the long-term task through to completion, and so cannot add it to his track record.

Americans can be impatient with long "learning curves" or extended training programs, because they may see them as preventing short-term achievement. Many American executives want their reading matter condensed into "executive summaries", and training programs chopped up into brief simplified bits of advice. Deeper understanding and the development of one's wisdom is sometimes sacrificed in favor of easily applicable "do's and don'ts" or lists of rules. One of the most popular management models in American for over two decades is the appropriately titled "One Minute Manager".

Lenore Madison has no hesitation about laying out her list of short-term accomplishments – whether they took her one minute, one month, or one year – and her rapid movement into jobs of successively greater responsibility. Her resume reflects the importance which both business organizations and their individual members, throughout their careers, attach to this.

Are you qualified?
American businesspeople are, of course, not the only ones who seek to meet objectives, and to do what needs to be done. But what makes Americans notable in this regard is that it is the core

of their professional self-esteem and day-to-day motivation. As we noted earlier, in America what is important is not whom you know or what you know. What matters is *what you do with what you know*. In business, your track record is more important than your education or other "qualifications".

On Lenore Madison's resume, did you note the absence of any description of her academic studies, apart from her BA (Bachelor of Arts) degree?

Traditionally, academic study has simply not been considered a vital ingredient of business success. It is true that in her field, more information on her studies of English literature would add little to our ability to judge her fitness for the kind of job she says she is looking for. In other fields, such as medicine, law, and other professions, more detail on university studies would be expected. But what is important here is the relative value that Americans give to the level and content of academic achievement, compared to common practice in other societies. The popular history of American business includes many examples of successful people who had no formal qualifications and little formal education, let alone a university degree. Yet they went on to develop successful products, establish companies, and – most important of all – acquire great wealth. The traditional ingredients for this dramatic success were (1) a good idea, and (2) hard work.

This does not mean, however, that American professionals and managers do not attach importance to a college or university degree. It is in fact considered indispensable, but – in the case of a BA or BS – primarily as a "door opener" or a jump onto the ladder of success, and as a general, if imperfect, indicator of intelligence and maturity. Lenore does hold a MBA (Master's Degree in Business Administration), which has doubtlessly given her a good basic knowledge of business, and to an employer evidence that her career aspirations no longer focus on Shakespeare. Yet even a MBA is not regarded as a "qualification" for any position, important credential though it may be, especially in marketing and financial services.

In this way, you can see that to an American, "Are you qualified?" does not mean, as it does in many countries, "Have you attained the right level of education or training?" It means rather "Do you have the combination of skills, training and record of similar accomplishment that enables you to do a job?" Is Lenore Madison "qualified" for a position in product marketing? According to the American way, and to her, she most definitely is, based on her "track record".

Keeping your options open

This emphasis on doing as opposed to learning in American business has another consequence for people's professional self-image which is important for non-Americans, especially those working in an American company, to understand. Since the American education system does not compel students to commit themselves very early to one special discipline, Americans are used to "keeping their options open" throughout their careers. We have seen the example of Lenore's BA degree in English literature. Irrespective of their academic field or vocational training, your American colleagues and "direct reports" are accustomed to looking "laterally" to other fields for opportunities for achievement and advancement – to move, for example, from finance to marketing, from technology to sales, from administration to logistics, and even from labor to management. In true American fashion, they view their field of opportunity as wide, and not limited or bound by their previous study or by the need to acquire the right "qualifications". They do not want to feel that they are being kept in a box.

If you are managing Americans, it will be useful to keep this in mind when learning about their career goals and expectations. As the title of a hit Broadway song goes, "Don't fence me in."

GETTING AHEAD – BLOWING YOUR OWN HORN

Lenore may have no problem seeing herself as "qualified" for the type of position she seeks, but she is also presenting herself, marketing herself, as such. Americans, as we saw in Chapter 3, learn to do this early in life. It is true that competition for employment is a fact of business life everywhere, not just in the USA. But if you come from a culture in which modesty is preferred, or talking about your accomplishments leaves a bad impression on others, be prepared for a different attitude among Americans.

We do not believe that our accomplishments will "speak for themselves". We have to speak for them, to "blow our own horn". Your American colleagues at work will keep "blowing", so to speak, throughout their time with the company. They want others to know what they are doing and have done, and want those achievements to be known to management. In her resume, Lenore makes no mention of others with whom she has worked, or the teams of which she was a member. This is not because she reached all those objectives by herself, or that she is ignoring the efforts of others. It is simply that she sees no need to mention them. She's blowing her horn; they are fully capable of blowing theirs.

"Looking out for number 1"

Lenore also knows that in American business life it is important to know what you want or to appear to know what you want. Americans do not expect their employer, however large, to fully manage their career development. Large Japanese companies, on the other hand, have traditionally adopted a much less autonomous and individualistic approach. In those organizations, one's career development is for the good of the company, not for the satisfaction of individual needs. It is the company that will largely determine the course of a person's career. Some large American organisations, such as IBM or General Motors, have had traditions of long-term corporate career development for employees. These tendencies, in both Japan and the USA are (I suspect) less strong now, with "leaner" organizations and more mobile employees. But whatever the corporate culture, an American knows that he can never keep a low profile or rest on his laurels if he expects to get ahead. A person is responsibility for his own career, and has to "look out for number 1".

Lenore may or may not be sure of what she wants, but she knows that it is important to give that impression. This is an essential factor to grasp when working with Americans. We will have more to say about this in Chapter 7. Between the lines, she is making very assertive statements in a very American style: I *want* to do this job; and I *am able* to do this job. You may find this to be egoistic, if not boastful. Perhaps she thinks too much of herself.

To Americans, however, she is doing no more than what is necessary to get ahead.

Work hard, play hard

Perhaps you observed that Lenore has made no mention of any aspect of her life outside of work (with the exception of the Junior League, which we will come to shortly). There is no mention of hobbies or personal interests. Does this leave her picture incomplete for you? Would you learn more about her as a complete person if you had this information? If you come from Europe or South America for example, Lenore may appear to be a capable but one-dimensional individual.

Many Americans, however, view this from a different angle. Lenore would feel that her hobbies or other "pastimes" are irrelevant to her abilities to do the job. By not mentioning them, she is implying that she would let nothing interfere with her commitment to the organization and to her work. At the office she will show that drive, commitment, and motivation through her activity level, and the hours she puts in from the start of her workday until she leaves. She will often have lunch at her desk, with little if any pause in her work.

Paradoxically, despite this work ethic of activity and performance, Americans are constantly reminded that work should be fun. Chief executives tell them that they should "have fun", while management gurus write books telling them how. Nobody is quite sure what "fun" means; perhaps it simply means avoiding depression or sadness. If you have fun while you work, in America you must also work hard to have fun. After work and on weekends, Americans will strive to be faithful to Benjamin

Franklin's creed by filling the time with activities, trying to be "efficient" and productive while supposedly enjoying "free time".

Lenore Madison is not likely to be an exception. If she has a family (also not mentioned on the resume), then non-work hours will be "quality time" with them. Perhaps her duties in the Junior League (an American volunteer service organization for women, not baseball for children!) occupy her. It is the one non-professional activity that she has mentioned on her resume. This is for two reasons. First, her responsibilities in the Junior League have called on skills relevant and similar to those required at work. Second, she wants to show that she has leadership capabilities within a group. Everything on her resume has one objective: to demonstrate her fitness for the job she seeks.

Are Americans "job-hoppers?"

What did you note about Lenore Madison's career progress? She may work hard and show commitment, but she has moved fairly rapidly from company to company, staying no more than two years at any one place. Does this seem to you to be evidence of instability? Disloyalty? Would you want to hire someone whose career history indicates that they will go somewhere else in a couple years?

Until quite recently, people from other countries looked upon Americans, comparatively, as "job-hoppers". Now, in the increasingly competitive and rapidly evolving world of international business, increasingly frequent job changes are becoming more common (and necessary) for professionals in many countries.

We need not concern ourselves here with what might be a "normal" length of time Americans stay in a job. That will vary with the industry sector, the type of company, economic conditions, and personal needs and preferences. Lenore Madison's movement from job to job is certainly not unusual, especially at the early stages of one's career. If she had been in the "dot.com" sector a few years ago, more than six months in one post might have been considered too long! Later in a person's career, the company retirement plan (pension) becomes a factor. It is natural for employees to want to remain longer with the company at that stage, the better to take advantage of it. Whatever the frequency, Americans expect this kind of self-initiated career mobility, as long as it results in a stronger track record, greater responsibilities, and the financial rewards that go with them.

During the time, however long, that Lenore is a member of an organization, she will work very hard for it, putting in long hours, supporting its objectives, believing in the value of its products and services. She will wear the company T-shirt or baseball cap. She will refer to the company CEO familiarly as "Charlie" (Yes, him again!). But when the opportunities for achievement and additional responsibility diminish, she will have no hesitation about looking elsewhere. Indeed, she may be continually looking for such opportunities both inside and outside the company while in her current post. What is more, her company knows and expects this.

"Goodbye" is not the hardest word...

In American business, the relationship between the employee and the organization is a calculative one, based on mutual self-interest. In exchange for her whole-hearted commitment, Lenore will expect, as we have seen, significant opportunities and a fair individual reward. The company, for its part, sees the relationship in a reciprocal way. It provides the opportunity in the form of a job function to be carried out and results to be attained. When the function or the results no longer fit the objectives of the organization, the job is eliminated, and with it the jobholder's employment.

This employer's prerogative, known in legal jargon as "employment at will", has in recent years been weakened by judicial decisions supportive of the employee's "property right" to the job. This has an important impact on the legality and appropriateness of certain management actions when it comes to "terminating" an employee, but does not change the underlying value shared by the two parties: when one no longer needs the other, there will be a parting of the ways.

This lack of long-term obligation also means that the parting can occur quickly, with little notice. This accounts for the view that American businesses operate with a "hire and fire" mentality. This view is oversimplified, as we shall see in Chapter 9. But both sides accept changes as necessary, desirable, and feasible. This is not to say that your American colleagues and business partners do not worry about job security, but they are accustomed to an economic climate of opportunity, in which the risk of losing one's job at relatively short notice is partly balanced by the likelihood of finding a new job shortly thereafter. This transition is, of course, more easily talked about than made. Generally speaking, however, it is made easier by a lighter burden of costs and regulations on companies, when it comes to taking on additional staff, compared to some other countries.

How do Americans feel about working for a foreign or foreign-owned company?

In the majority of cases, they will feel no differently than if they were working for an American employer, provided that the opportunities for achievement and advancement are there. Some may not even be aware that their company, perhaps with a well recognized trademark or brand, is foreign-owned.

At more senior levels of management, however, they may have more apprehensions. They may be worried about being far from the centres of power, decision-making, and information. They may feel very uncomfortable as the "foreigners" in the group, something to which they are not at all accustomed, especially if they have spent most of their careers with American companies.

If you are recruiting Americans to key management positions, this question should be an important part of a selection interview. You can attract capable people by means of high pay, but you will have little chance of retaining them if their needs are not met.

"Lenore Madison" does not exist. Her profile, however, is neither caricature nor exaggeration. It is, in fact, a typical expression of the attitudes and expectations of job and career that your American colleagues, bosses, and partners carry throughout their working lives.

And she doesn't work for free...

MOTIVATING AMERICANS – IS IT THE MONEY?

What sort of rewards or compensation does Lenore Madison

expect for all her accomplishments and individual contribution. "Americans think only about money", you may say, knowing that we probably think about other things too. Yet money is very important for some reasons common to many people around the world, and for other reasons particularly applicable to Americans.

Poverty is a bad idea
American attitudes towards money and wealth in general are based on four assumptions.

First, this large expansive country is regarded as a "land of opportunity". This description is both mythical – for some have been excluded from this opportunity – and practical. Its positive tone implies that one's goals are achievable, and that there is sufficient opportunity, in the form of freedom and resources, for all. This American world-view contrasts with that in many other parts of the world, which holds that the amount of "opportunity" is limited and needs to be distributed rather than created. Americans, on the other hand, believe that when a person enriches himself, that enrichment, in most cases, does not come at someone else's expense. Put in simpler terms: "Just because I win, that does not mean that you or someone else loses."

Entrepreneurialism has always been a good thing in America. Freed from Europe's strict monopolistic guild systems and its class-based distribution of wealth, people in America have striven to enrich themselves, and by doing do, enrich others. Entrepreneurs have never been viewed as "cowboys" (an expression common to our British friends), as threats to the established order.

Second, wealth is still regarded as a reward for hard work, good ideas, and risk-taking – for entrepreneurialism if you like. Americans accept wide differences in salary level between junior clerk and vice president, provided those differences fairly reflect differences in contribution and responsibility. We also accept wide differences between people in their personal wealth, again provided that the difference is a function of the wealth they have created, responsibilities held, or value provided.

In the last couple of years, there has been concern expressed in America at levels of executive compensation, largely in response to financial accounting malpractices in several large companies. Yet Americans, compared to people in many other countries, do not complain constantly about "fat cats". They neither admire nor resent the rich, nor do they assume that wealth means greed. An opinion poll in 1998 found that 50 percent of Americans believed that there was the "right amount" of rich people in the country. Twenty percent even felt that there were too few! Perhaps this attitude toward the rich reflects the average American's optimism about the chances of joining them. When asked, in a different poll, "Do you think it is still possible to start out poor in this country, work hard, and become rich?" 84 percent said yes.[1]

Third, enriching oneself in America is to some extent a "social" responsibility, however paradoxical that may appear. At a basic level, Americans need money to pay for things that in other countries are provided by the state and funded through taxation, such as university education and medical insurance. To not look after yourself and your immediate family in this way is to make yourself a burden to the state, or to other members of your family. We should not exaggerate the vulnerability of Americans.

The government, at the federal and state levels, provides considerable social welfare and medical benefits to certain segments of the population, such as the poor or the elderly. More affluent Americans are able to take advantage of tax relief or other specific benefits as much as they can. If they are employees, they will certainly want to enjoy the benefits of their company's medical insurance and retirement plan (if it is large enough to have one). The state pension (known as Social Security) is not likely to be sufficient for the lifestyle to which they look forward.

While Americans need to provide for themselves in this way, their wealth, or what remains after taxation, is normally reinvested in the economy, through home ownership and investments in stocks and shares.

Yet to an American money means far more than this basic foundation of sufficiency and protection. It means independence and greater control over one's life, without which, individualism would, to an American, be meaningless. This leads us to the **fourth factor** in Americans' views of wealth and enrichment: money brings with it the means to exercise *choice*.

A common situation of daily management may help to illustrate this.

EXAMPLE 5.2

Let us suppose that in your country, or in the business environment you are accustomed to, an employee has earned an individual reward for an excellent piece of work. You ask the employee to choose one of three rewards: (a) three days' paid time off from work; (b) a three-day training seminar or professional conference, at company expense and the employee's preference; (c) a bonus payment equivalent to three days' work.

How might an employee in your culture respond?

◆ This problem would never appear. Where I come from, we avoid giving individual rewards, preferring to give only group rewards to maintain solidarity, teamwork, and fairness.

◆ He would be more likely to choose the seminar or conference.

◆ He would be more likely to choose the time off.

◆ He would be more likely to choose the money.

If you answered (**a**), then be prepared for very different expectations in America.
Perhaps you answered (**b**) or (**c**), as indicative of the values of people in your part of the business world.

If the employee were American, he might do the same. This would depend of course on the individual's needs. But while an American may talk a great deal about "work-life balance" (**a**) or "professional growth" (**b**) as important factors in job satisfaction, they would be more likely to choose the money. Why? Primarily because the money means that the person can then choose the *end* reward, the benefit that the money will bring. In America, there is abundant choice, and to many people, freedom means the freedom to choose. With the money, one can exercise that freedom. Neither the range nor the quality of the available alternatives is relevant. *What is important is the feeling of control and independence that comes with having the choice.*

The 'bottom line'

So what does it take to motivate Americans? The first element is an opportunity to achieve, to build a track record, through the accomplishment of clear short-term objectives. The second is individual reward *linked to performance*. Lenore Madison will indeed be motivated by money, provided it is a fair individual reward for specific achievement. Current management jargon refers to this as "pay for performance". It is not the whole answer to the question of compensation: fair basic salary policies, generous benefits, and group incentives are also important. But the "bottom line" is, "Pay me for what I achieve, not for who I am."

At this stage, you may be asking yourself, "But how can such an individual ever work as part of a team, or fit into an organization?"

The short answer is: very willingly. Let us look more closely at the American way of teamwork, participation and management.

6

"My Way or the Highway"!: Management and Teamwork with Americans

A non-American who has dealings with or who joins "corporate America" will find many familiar concepts and structures. Americans have been preaching management ideals and ideas for years, and for an equally long period, writers, consultants, and businesspeople have been imitating, disseminating, or criticising them. But as with other aspects of working with Americans, it is the day-to-day assumptions, expectations, and behavior that can present problems and obstacles to the foreigner.

POWER, ACCOUNTABILITY AND HIERARCHY

Our look at the American way of management, leadership, and teamwork starts at the top.

Basic fact: senior American management are primarily accountable to the owners of the business. In many smaller businesses, the owner is also the chief executive. Most ownership is by shareholders (also known in the USA as *stockholders*), who – more than in any other country – consist of the public, either individually or through collective investment funds. In America, the prevailing ownership pattern does not involve banks, other companies, or the government as much as is the case elsewhere. This fundamental accountability to the public as owners (hence the American designation, *public* company) is the most powerful factor in the way the business is run. Profit is the means to the end of increasing the wealth of those stockholders, either through distributed dividends or an increase in share value. But profit is also viewed by American management as a means to a higher end. In the words of one senior executive:

> *While the return of profit to our shareholders is not the sole justification for our existence as a business enterprise, it is the indispensable means without which we cannot make a contribution to society.*[1]

In American business, profit is not the *reward* for service to society, profit is the *means* by which service is rendered, creating wealth for owners, employees, and society at large. We have seen this value expressed before, in Chapter 5, in the individual American's attitude toward wealth and money.

In a society of few obligations, one that is mentioned particularly by American executives is that of "our obligation to our shareholders". It may be the only one. Indeed, American management feels little obligation or need to take into account the needs of other so-called "stakeholders" in the business. The differences with continental Europe, for example, are striking. American companies as a rule do not have "advisory boards", "works councils", or mandatory participation by employees on the Board of Directors (although there are exceptional cases of each of these). Even labor unions have relatively little power in the private sector. Relations between unions and employers are in any case adversarial, so conflict resolution starts with that assumption.

But while top management's freedom of action is not constrained by those factors, their accountability is both strict and short-term. From quarter to quarter, shareholders expect an increase in their wealth, or at the very least an improvement in company results. When the disappointment of shareholders is combined with press and media criticism, top management are normally quick to respond. The popular and business media in America are free and powerful; American executives fear bad publicity as much as bad results. Both cause the stock price to drop, and can make recruitment and retention of staff much harder.

While American senior management wields considerable authority on behalf of the company and its shareholders, an executive's title Figure 6.1 is not necessarily an indicator of his power. That will depend on the amount of the business (budget allocation, revenue, number of employees) under that person's control. All executive vice-presidents (EVPs) may report directly to the CEO, but the EVP Human Resources is not likely to have as much power as, for example, the EVP Finance or Marketing. An EVP of "Special Projects" may have a relatively small amount or organizational resources under his control, and thus have less scope for the exercise of direct personal authority.

THE THREE P's – PROCESS, PROGRAMS, PREACHING

How do American senior executives whatever their power, view their jobs? What are they supposed to *do*? That question has a simple, but not easy, answer: their job is to *get results*. In other words, they strive to reach targets.

That is not news to anyone. But non-Americans may be struck by

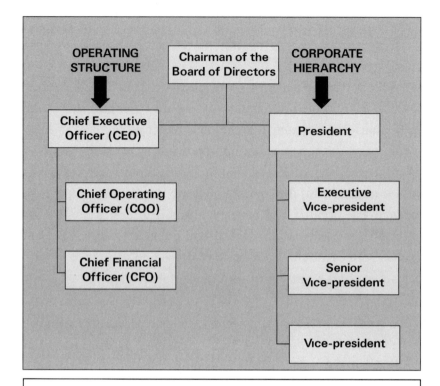

Notes:

Titles in the operating structure are found in both public and privately held companies. The titles of corporate hierarchy tend to be found principally in public companies.

The operating structure may also include such designations as Chief Information Officer (CIO) and, more rarely, Chief Human Resources Officer.

The same person does not normally hold the positions of Chairman and Chief Executive Officer in larger public companies. In smaller companies or privately held companies, the same individual may take both roles.

The positions of CEO and President are often combined. The CFO will normally be some sort of vice-president.

The various vice-presidential titles establish a rank order in the company. An executive vice-president may or may not sit on the Executive (or Management) Committee led by the CEO.

The President of a subsidiary may also be a vice-president of the parent company.

Figure 6.1. Executive titles, roles and rank.

the methods that American executives prefer to use in achieving these. To use a sometimes irritating mnemonic device that is much loved by senior managers and consultants, we will refer to the most important of these as the "Three P's": Process, Programs, and Preaching.

Process

Without entering the age-old discussion as to whether management is an art or a science, we can say that for generations, American business has studied, analyzed, compared, and most of all, talked about management. Americans are particularly fond of describing management in terms of processes – a system of steps that effect sequential change: the "decision-making process," the "performance management process", "business process re-engineering", the "total quality management" process, the "project management process", even the "creative process". This belief in process enables the process of management to be not only described and studied, but also taught and learned. When management becomes learnable, it becomes more democratic, not in style, but in accessibility and applicability to anyone anywhere. American business has been teaching others, or trying to, at least since the end of the Second World War, when it sought to help war-ravaged western European industries recover their productivity.

But at an organizational level, for a process to be "implemented", American executives like to rely on the second "P" – programs.

Programs

America is a land of wonders, in which everything is in constant motion and every change seems an improvement. The idea of novelty is there indissolubly connected with the idea of amelioration.

Alexis de Tocqueville[2]

A *program*, in American business, is an organized campaign to bring about some kind of change, usually based on some *process*. A program is often given a memorable and supposedly catchy title, such as "Enterprise 2005" or "Road to Excellence", or something similar. A senior executive, sometimes the CEO, is designated as the leader or sponsor. Meetings are held, and internal or external publicity is generated to inform lower level managers and employees about the goals and tasks that will bring about the changes that are envisioned.

This way of bringing about change is not unique to business, or to American business. It does, however, embody certain important American values and assumptions. The first, as observed by De Tocqueville, is that change is a good thing. It can of course be a bad thing, in the form of deterioration or degradation, but Americans attach relatively less importance to stability than do many people elsewhere in the world, and so they do not instinctively fear change. If you listed among your perceptions of Americans in Chapter 2, "open to new ideas", you have put your finger on this.

Change brings about something new, and newness is another good thing. "Progress is our most important product" was the motto of the General Electric Corporation some years ago. It may be less fashionable now to talk about material progress as an undiluted benefit, but in the American pursuit of ideals and achievements, change, newness, and improvement are necessary.

A third important American assumption here is if change is necessary, it does not need to be "evolutionary". To use another American business cliché, it needs to be "revolutionary". Change is something that you "drive", rapidly, visibly and concretely, and with leadership. That is where the third "P", Preaching, comes in.

Preaching

The word *preach*, drawn from the domain of religion, defines very clearly a style of executive leadership that is very common in American business, but often incomprehensible to many non-Americans. If you have been working in a foreign subsidiary of an American corporation, you have at some point probably had to put up with "mission statements" and lists of "core values" (such as Innovation, Close to the Customer, Communication, etc.). These appear in company literature, on the corporate website, in new employee handbooks and on posters affixed to walls and partition dividers from Chicago to China. The popularity of these methods of implementing programs, or of creating a "corporate culture", stems from the management literature of the 1980s, in which American corporations were criticized for having lost their sense of "mission" or purpose, their focus.

Whether or not mission statements and statements of "core values" and "key drivers" are effective in achieving the desired ends is another question best left to management consultants. It is easy to be cynical about them, which is always the case when a person, an organization, or (especially) a nation articulates ideals, and then inevitably falls short of realizing them. Non-Americans may perceive them as naïve, unrealistic or even patronising.

EXAMPLE 6.2

One German manager described for me her reaction to seeing "Quality" listed among her company's most important "core values".

"Why do they have to say this?" she lamented. "Don't they realize that as Germans this is already part of us, of who we are?"

In this example, the German's reaction was a common one to what appears to be an American need to state the obvious. She implied that if Americans have to spell out the importance of quality in this way, then it must be lacking in them and in their business. Other non-Americans, however, may respond differently. A Frenchman working in a hotel near Paris was delighted that his establishment had been purchased by an American company and was now part of a chain. "The Americans know how to develop an *esprit de corps*," he declared.

Effective or ineffective, these practices echo American attitudes and customs from the early days of the settlement of the continent and the establishment of a new society, when preachers were both the spiritual and intellectual leaders of their communities. Armed with "mission statements" it is no accident that many American chief executives become "missionaries", preaching every sort of ideal, from ending world poverty through the internet, to saving the planet, or achieving success through their approach to management.

Modelled on traditional religious practices, and shaped to fit the requirements of secular business life, mission and values statements are necessary American tools for giving to a diverse group of people a sense of common purpose, and on a practical level, providing a basis for daily actions. We like these things to be made explicit, preferably in writing, so that everyone can pull together.

If you sympathize with our German friend and find this sort of corporate preaching tiresome and unnecessary, many Americans would agree, especially if they cannot relate it to the job that needs to be done. But we are used to it, we respond to it, and we expect it. We will certainly notice if it is absent, and may wonder why. We are not a cynical people by nature (although we can find plenty of things to be cynical about). We appreciate strong corporate leadership providing clear direction, under the influence of a strong visible chief.

What about "People"?

If you have entered into the spirit of this "Three P's" format, you are probably complaining at this point that we have omitted the most important P – people. American senior managers would agree, and no doubt would have added that to the list in answer to the question, "What do you need in order to get results?"

"People are the leaders of change", would serve as a good statement of the ideal of executive leadership. (People are also supposed to be the followers, although that may be a less inspirational way of looking at it.) Americans expect that top management will want to make changes, not only to better achieve results, but so that an executive can put his particular "stamp" on an organization. In many American companies, large, medium, or small, there still exists a very real respect for the values and personality of the founder. In many cases, of course, that influence is sustained directly in the person of the founder as CEO or Chairman of the Board. In older companies, the influence of the founding "entrepreneur with a vision" may still be strong, unless corporate mergers and take-overs have erased it.

For the most part, however, Americans will not look to the past for that inspiration. Businesses are constantly changing, with or without programs, and customers' needs are changing as well. Americans look to the present, to their current senior management, for leadership.

Let us now turn our attention to the middle and lower levels of the organization. How do Americans view their relationship to this hierarchy and to their immediate boss?

THE "DIRECT REPORT"

"I work for Susan Johnson."

"He reports to John Hirsch."

"The Vice President of Finance has six direct reports."

These ways of expressing one's relationship to one's boss may seem strange to you. After all, an employee of an organization does not "work for" a single person (except in cases of a two-person company). He works for the organisation. And why refer to people as "reports"? Why not just say "subordinates"? (Perhaps you thought a report was a kind of document or presentation.)

The fact is that Americans use the term "subordinates" less and less, because it implies inferior status, something that we egalitarian Americans can never admit that we accept. But "direct report" is a useful term, expressing as it does two key aspects of a relationship: the directness, which means one-to-one without intermediaries or barriers of rank; and the reporting, which is what a "subordinate" must above all do to his manager.

Do you perceive Americans as "hierarchical" or "following the chain of command", or do you, conversely, perceive them as people who often bypass the chain of command and disagree with their managers? I have often encountered these contrasting views on the part of non-Americans. Your particular view will depend on your background, but both have some truth in them. This is explained by the particular American formula of relating to one's manager, which balances attentiveness to his requirements with a need for autonomy and independence.

Separating personal from professional

The first important aspect of this formula is that the manager–direct report relationship (or boss–subordinate relationship if you prefer) does not in any way apply away from work, or in matters not pertaining to work. The people involved may go to sporting events together, get together with their families, and may even be friends. Their working relationship is completely separate from their personal relationship. The manager is not entitled to any special treatment, respect, or regard away from work.

The American manager is therefore not a person of different social rank or type. Nor is he regarded as a "father figure" (and I use the term here to include women, without feeling obliged to say "mother figure"). An American worker does not expect his boss to help with personal problems, by offering, for example, financial assistance, counselling, or even an "ear" to confide in. The first of these is considered very bad practice, and American organizations frown upon it or may indeed prohibit it. For the second, many large American companies expect troubled employees to be referred to, or to refer themselves to "employee assistance" services. As for a trusting ear in which to confide, this might occur but will depend on the relationship between the two. Work and non-work issues are kept separate, for it is work that really matters.

"One-on-one"

When an American says that he "works for Susan Johnson", he is implying that he has a one-to-one relationship with that person. The manager is not only or even primarily a team leader; he or she is also an individual leader, within certain limits and with certain definite responsibilities.

To start with, an American assumes that his boss has certain clearly defined objectives of her own, which represent "pieces" of the overall company goals. Through this system of delegated authority, the direct report accepts and expects that he will support his manager's objectives. For this reason, the two need to be in full agreement as to the direct report's objectives. Americans define job expectations primarily in this way, and do not rely on written job descriptions or professional obligations.

Managers, for their part, are expected to take responsibility for the feedback, evaluation, and development of the performance of their direct reports. This is not to say that American managers always carry out these responsibilities well, or at all. These tasks are not easy, and many managers do their best to avoid them. This accounts for the need and popularity of such theories as the "One-Minute Manager" mentioned earlier. It is also true that the higher the level of management, the less "developmental" is the relationship. Nevertheless, even upper management complain that they do not get enough feedback from their chiefs. In short, throughout the organization Americans will expect more from their managers than just to be "left to get on with" the job.

Like anyone else, Americans do want a degree of autonomy. They do not always expect or want to be told what to do or how to do it. The direct-reporting relationship does not mean that control is expected to be tight. Control (in the *English* sense of the word – direction, correction, feedback) should be as tight or loose as it needs to be for the job to be done, and ideally agreed between the people involved.

WHEN IS MY BOSS NOT MY BOSS?

With those elements in place, an American can be comfortable with two variations to this structure: "matrix" or "dotted line" reporting, and bypassing laterally or vertically the chain of command.

Matrix reporting
Matrix management evolved as a way of managing operational and project responsibilities for certain objectives, while maintaining an overall corporate structure and accountability. Under this arrangement, one manager provides specific day-to-day direction to an employee on his immediate assignment, a project for example. The employee's "direct" manager retains responsibility for his training, career development, conditions of

employment, and overall role within the organization. (See figure 6.3.) This appears to be a case of two bosses, but is more accurately described as two separate roles. There may be conflicts, and some organizations are not able to make this work. But provided that the specific responsibilities of each "line" are made clear, Americans can work effectively in this structure. To them, management and authority reside **in the role, not in the person**.

Bypassing the boss

Americans do not expect that their managers will have all the answers to organizational and technical questions, nor are they expected to be able to provide all the resources necessary for a particular job. For their part, managers in general understand that their direct reports will have greater knowledge than they of situational requirements and methods for doing a given job. For these reasons, an American will normally go *directly* to others in the organization from whom he needs information, co-operation or resources. It will not be necessary to go through his boss or to involve him. It is definitely expected, however, that he will keep his boss informed of the "bypass".

On the other hand, it may *not* be appropriate to bypass one's manager in cases of grievance or dissatisfaction. These cases do occur, when a person has a poor relationship with his boss or when he wants to "blow the whistle", in other words, to report business practices contrary to corporate policy or ethics. (This is not to be confused with blowing one's horn!) A poor relationship with one's boss, of course, makes it necessary to bypass him in order to communicate with someone else. But in the majority of these cases, senior management (or the Legal or Human Resources department) will still expect the matter to first be

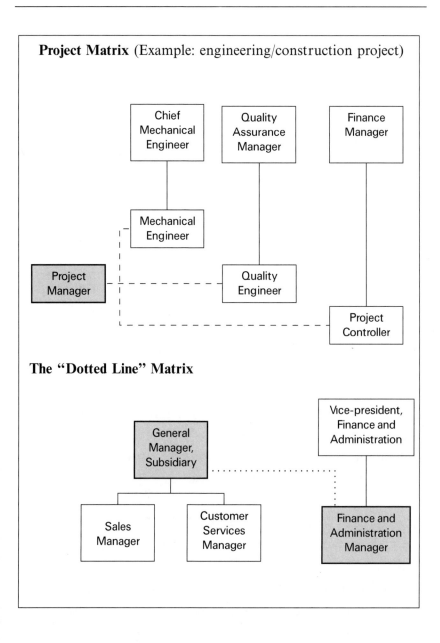

Figure 6.3. The Matrix Recalled.

discussed with one's immediate manager. *"If you have a problem, first talk to your boss."*

TO "MBO" OR NOT TO "MBO" – AMERICAN MANAGEMENT STYLE

What sort of management style are Americans comfortable with? It is even more difficult than normal to offer generalities here; this depends on the people involved. Americans expect their managers to be flexible, adapting their degree of control to the demands of the task, and to the skills and motivation of the individual.

We can say that Americans expect to have specific measurable objectives toward which to direct their efforts. Whether these objectives are set by their management, or jointly agreed, is less important – the key is the target. In the light of this, and of Lenore Madison's expectations, you can see now why Management by Objectives (popularly known as MBO), or should we say the MBO process, has played such a big part in American management. As a formal process or "program", it has perhaps fallen out of fashion, but this focus on objectives, on results, is virtually taken for granted in America.

What has been your experience with MBO? How widely has MBO been used in your country or your organization?

To ilustrate of the difficulties other business cultures may have with MBO, one intercultural specialist, Geert Hofstede, has pointed to the example of France. Known in that country as *la gestion participative par objectifs*, it had relatively little success when it was introduced. The explanation proposed by Hofstede is that the theoretically "participative" aspect of it ran counter to French notions of hierarchical authority, or in his words, "power distance".[3]

In other business cultures, MBO has had varying degrees of relevance, popularity, and effectiveness. In America, the degree of "co-determination" of objectives on the part of manager and direct report is less than we would like to think, but the principle has an egalitarian appeal. Americans expect to have a certain degree of "input" concerning their objectives, but they also accept that these often depend on higher level departmental or corporate objectives on which they will have no say.

In American business, a productive management style is more than just a matter of setting objectives. Americans expect a certain amount of feedback from their boss. They will also want, up to a point, to be recognized when they have done a good job. Perhaps more than many Europeans, we appreciate a certain amount of direct praise. If we do not receive any, we will feel the need to blow our own horn even louder. And perhaps more than some Asians or Latin Americans, we are comfortable with that recognition being addressed to us individually, and not only to the group of which we are a part.

PLAYING IN THE BAND – TEAMWORK THE AMERICAN WAY

At this stage, you may be wondering how it is possible to integrate these individualistic self-interested Americans into a team. We Americans think of ourselves as good co-operative team members by nature and would point to the success of American businesses as evidence. That self-image is, however, a reflection of our particular view of teamwork.

Far from resisting working in a team, Americans embrace it, as long as it matches our expectations. We know that without it, we cannot achieve organizational objectives. That is why organizations exist, after all. But what carries equal weight to Americans is the expectation that a good team, at organizational or project level, will make possible the individual achievement that they seek.

What are the qualities of a good team member, from an American perspective?

WYSIWYG – what you see is what you get!

Let us return to the example of Lenore Madison (Figure 5.1). Her resume gives us no indication of the quality of her teamwork, or of how she might fit productively into a team. Would she be compatible or incompatible with the others? We are unable to get even the slightest idea of her personality or her individuality from her resume.

Her response to this would be, "What you see here is what you get!" She would remind you that, "I am what I do." Her 'personality' is the results-oriented worker you see. Her individuality at work is the individualism of personal achievement, not the uniqueness of her ideas, her self-expression, or her personal "style".

This is a very different view to that of other business cultures – possibly yours – in which building a good team depends on finding different complementary and compatible personalities who can fit together or "harmonize".

Choosing to fit in

To Americans, fitting in is a matter of what one *does*, not what one *is*. If you asked Lenore, "How well do you fit into a team?" she might find the question strange. Her reply would be that she does what is necessary and expected in order to fit into the team. She will, in essence, *make herself fit in*. She knows that it is expected of her, and sees no need to mention it on her resume. Personality is not that important. As a team member, she will adopt the "personality" that is necessary to support the team and get the job done. She will fit in because she chooses to, not because she is a certain type of person.

The most important criterion, therefore, for the selection of team members is *not* personality, or thinking style, but rather the ability to do a required task. Team harmony is above all assured, not by having people who get along with each other, important though that is, but by first having a clear framework of goals, objectives, job roles and responsibilities. Good relationships will in part be the *result* of task clarity, rather than its *cause*. Teamwork is yet another application of that fundamental principle of working with Americans: whether we are buyer and seller, or manager and direct report, our relationship ultimately depends on how well we can get things done together.

This attitude may explain why, to some business people from outside the USA, "corporate" Americans may appear to be such conformists.

In this very gray area of teamwork, we have emphasized possible group differences in order to delineate them with sharper lines. The foundations of successful teamwork are the same everywhere: clear objectives, roles, responsibilities, communication, and good relationships between the team members. Americans do not want to work in teams that are bureaucracies. Like others, they want to work with congenial colleagues.

It goes without saying that getting along well facilitates the quick resolution of conflicts, whatever their origin, and prevents others. At the same time, those good relationships are not just a matter of a bunch of people having pizza and beer together. They depend, in the American view, on a clear framework. For this reason, Americans often work well with more formalized team "processes", such as various project management methodologies or group problem-solving and brain-storming methods.

What does this mean for you?

Here is what Americans are likely to expect from you as the leader of an American team, or of an international team that includes Americans:

♦ They expect an active leader, not one who will merely "let them get on with it". An active team leader will give the group focus, by means of a "mission" (at an organizational level) or simply a clear common objective, feedback on progress, and a positive confident attitude.

In the absence of clear leadership, Americans are likely to view their own areas of contribution as most important, and give priority to those. They may be reluctant to "take a back seat" to let someone else "drive", if they have no confidence in the driver. Consequently, they may either turn away from the team goal in favour of their own individual objectives, or they may attempt to assert leadership on their own.

◆ They may expect that the team leader will play a role in resolving disagreements, since these often stem, in the American view, from task issues rather than "personality questions".

Your preferred style may be to expect the people involved to negotiate a solution among themselves. If you select team members for their ability to get along together, they should as professionals be able to sort things out. In many situations, this approach may be appropriate. But Americans often see something more at stake here than "getting along". If their individual contributions are at issue, then they are not as likely to set their differences aside "for the good of the team", precisely because as we have seen, these contributions are *part of* the "good of the team".

Having looked at these American assumptions and expectations of teamwork, it is time that we observed an American team in action (or inaction, as the case may be), as described in Example 6.4. This raises a number of questions that relate to the American way of meetings, team problem-solving, group decision-making, and relationship to the hierarchy.

EXAMPLE 6.4

Neptune Multi+Physics Corporation is a multi-national scientific instruments company based in Austin, Texas. The company is developing a new financial management system, intended to track sales, cost of sales, cost of goods, pricing, and sales incentives by product, country and customer. Senior management have decided that the system will be developed and first implemented in the USA, after which it will then be "rolled out" to all of NM+P's subsidiaries worldwide.

Budget for this project is under the North American Regional Finance department, while the corporate Information Systems Group (ISG) in Austin has primary responsibility for development.

A project review meeting is taking place at an important early stage of the project. The purpose of the meeting is to review the scope of the project, users' requirements, and the schedule.

The participants are:

♦ Project Manager, assigned to this project from the Finance Department

♦ Systems Development Manager, from ISG

♦ Business Analyst, reporting to the Systems Development (SD) Manager

♦ Three Systems Programmers, also reporting to the SD Manager

♦ Vice President Finance: North American Operations, the senior manager present.

The overall structure looks like this:

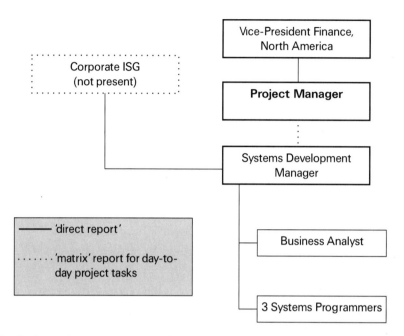

The Business Analyst and the senior Systems Programmer are convinced that the current plan – completion of phase 1 in six months, and the three months pilot testing – is unrealistic and impossible to achieve, given the workload and level of technical skill within the project team. They believe that if the company wishes to meet the schedule, it should purchase a commercially developed system, such as those offered by various systems software companies, and work with the vendor to adapt it to NM+P's requirements.

During the meeting, the Project Manager refers to the planned schedule several times. Neither the Business Analyst, nor the senior Systems Programmer, nor anyone else, makes any objections or expresses any opinions concerning the realism of the plan.

1. *Based on your background and business experience*, what is your opinion of the lack of discussion?

a) The lack of discussion is understandable, since neither the Project Manager nor the Vice President Finance has yet invited people to express their views.

b) The lack of discussion makes no sense. Surely the reason to hold such a meeting is to identify potential problems and decide what to do about them.

c) The lack of discussion is not a problem. Meetings like this are not the right place for expressing these sorts of disagreements or concerns.

d) The lack of discussion indicates poor leadership. All those present should have the opportunity to express their opinions of the plan at the meeting. If the plan has been decided by management, the whole group should nevertheless accept it.

e) The lack of discussion is understandable. Project plans are guidelines, not firm commitments, so concern about achieving the plan is a low priority.

f) The lack of discussion indicates that even though they have their doubts, the team accept and will work toward the schedule, which is what they should do.

g) Other. *If you have an opinion that is not described by the above alternatives, you can note it here:*

2. Considering the list of alternatives, what do you think would be the view of an American?

Before we comment on your response and the American expectations of such a situation, we need to point out that this is not intended to illustrate a "typical" situation in American business. Things may or may not happen in this way. Many such meetings involving Americans would differ greatly according to circumstances. But many Americans would not be surprised or even disappointed by what is described here, and it will be helpful to understand why.

But first, what does your response tell you about your expectations in this situation? Compare it to how an American might view each alternative:

Alternative (a)
Not applicable here, normally. If certain participants had wanted to express their views, they would not feel that they had to wait for an invitation.

However, they might be cautious in expressing their concerns, for a number of reasons that we will cover shortly.

Alternative (b)
Many Americans would agree with this. But many others would feel that in fact a meeting is not the best place or means for problem-solving and decision-making. That should be done by those directly involved, those who "own" (are responsible for) the problem.

Alternative (c)
Many Americans would agree with this statement, and we discuss this further below.

Alternative (d)
This would not be the usual American expectation. That a plan has been decided by management does not mean that it cannot be changed, but there is a "right" way to go about this.
Furthermore, to use the meeting simply as an occasion for people

to let off steam – which does happen – would be considered a waste of time.

Alternative (e)
Americans generally do not look at schedules as mere "guidelines". They represent commitments, a kind of contract. The schedule may be changed, but the Americans will focus their efforts on the objective with a positive, but not naïve, attitude.

Alternative (f)
Silence does not mean consent. As we noted, people may for certain reasons hold back their opinions at this point. The project team members do, however, recognize that the objective has been set by upper management.

So why, then, might Americans not express their doubts about the schedule?

Wrong time, wrong place
The first and more important reason is that, in fact, a project review meeting may not be the best occasion for this. The basic American assumption would be that those members of the project team responsible for developing the schedule would take it upon themselves to meet together and develop a solution. They would not necessarily expect to consult with other members of the project team who were not involved in planning. To use a common American expression, because they are responsible for the schedule, they "own" it. Their meeting, moreover, would have a very different atmosphere to the one described here: full exchanges of opinion, strong arguments as to what is best, equally strong disagreements with others' views. It would conclude with a

clear agreement on what is to be done, by whom, and when.

Having prepared a solution, they would then inform the rest of the project team, and present it to the Project Manager. If it turned out that higher level approvals were needed, the Project Manager would in turn present the revised schedule to upper management, according to the chain of command.

The Americans' objective will be to persuade others of the best possible solution, given the requirements and resources. They will *not* simply seek to agree on a course of action that "everyone can live with", in which all the different points of view are accommodated. In the opinion of some American managers, getting everyone to agree is what is meant by "consensus", but it is really a question of persuasion.

Wrong people

A second reason for the lack of discussion has to do with the presence of the regional Vice President of Finance, the Project Manager's boss. To bring up questions about the plan at this point might embarrass the Project Manager (or even the Systems Development Manager), if he is not aware of these, or if he has not previously discussed them with the VP. Whatever they may think of their boss, the members of the team will not do that. Furthermore, the VP is not likely to want to hear about problems with the schedule unless the Project Manager or the team is ready to present a solution.

Wrong attitude

These are the two other factors that may also influence people's behaviour in this situation.

The first is more a matter of particular corporate culture than of American culture. It is an unstated norm in some organizations to set "aggressive" targets, with the equally unstated expectation that they will not be one hundred percent achieved. But it is often better to attempt and fall short, provided one has an explanation and a solution for the shortfall (or someone else to blame), than to be timid in setting the target. Trial-and-error is better than a risk avoidance approach of exhaustive time-consuming detailed planning. There will always be a need for balance, but this attitude is common in American business, and non-Americans need to be aware of this. "Aggressive" targets are motivators, and are evidence of a positive attitude. Caution, however logical, sensible and rational, is not rewarded.

Indeed the project plan may be one of the Vice President of Finance's own individual objectives, achievement of which would affect his individual bonus. Nobody is going to want to appear to be an obstacle to *that,* unless it is the VP's own boss.

The second factor also has to do with positive attitudes. To be a "team player" in American business means more than simply working hard toward a common goal. It means that a person will **"disagree and commit"** – set aside his own opinion to support the course of action determined by the management or by the group. Americans will not try too hard to patch things up, to find a compromise, to let a dissenter "save face", or to win an opponent over with further argument. Therefore, in practical terms, expressing concerns or doubts without offering a solution, being cynical, pushing one's arguments or criticism too far, or opting out are very bad form. They are "not an option".

In this case, therefore, the team members may be keeping their opinions to themselves until a practical, feasible and permissible alternative is available. In the meantime, it is better to show public support for the team with expressions of optimism and confidence, or simply by restraining their doubts or scepticism.

What can we offer then as general guidelines for the American way of holding meetings and making decisions together?

PURPOSES OF MEETINGS

Americans are less inclined than, say, many northern Europeans, to view meetings as a setting for making decisions. One American chief executive had a memo sent to managers saying "Staff meetings are not the place to make decisions!" Americans are more comfortable with a more individualized approach – those with direct responsibility address the problem together.

In American business culture, there is much talk of consensus, but little tradition of collective decision-making and none of collective responsibility. Moreover, there is little expectation in American business culture of consultation per se. It's not that American colleagues and managers will not consult others. It is rather that they will not do this as a matter of course, but only when necessary and then only with those directly involved. To use a phrase we have used several times already, *they will not feel obliged.* Individuals are expected to own fully their objectives and tasks, and to obtain the support of others through persuasion rather than through consultation. Americans' distrust of "collective" decision-making is based on the belief that it often results in a weak decision. Many American management training courses strive to convince them otherwise, but with limited success.

Americans will see meetings (or video-conferences) as opportunities to inform and be informed, to be visible and make one's efforts visible to others; in short to "stay in the loop", and avoid isolation from others.

CONDUCT OF MEETINGS

Here again, standard good practice, as described in management books, prescribes the preparation of a detailed agenda and adherence to proper techniques for leading the meeting. But do not expect your American colleagues to be too formal or strict in adhering to these.

Americans do expect that people will speak up if they wish to. Keeping quiet means that you have nothing to say. A certain amount of social talk or even a bit of letting off steam is tolerated. But any apparent lack of focus or objective in a meeting may cause an American participant to use the opportunity to advance his own "agenda", or to simply tune out. Unfortunately, skilled discussion leaders are hard to find in American organizations. This can be frustrating enough for American participants, but doubly so for international colleagues.

We can go only so far in attempting to generalize about American patterns and preferences in these areas of teamwork, meetings and decision-making. So much depends on the character of the particular organization and people involved. Much of what we have described here is more often seen in large organizations, whether multi-national or not. Smaller companies will have a very different feel or atmosphere: a greater sense of urgency, closer relationships between company managers and their "colleagues", fewer formal management systems, greater visibility of success or failure.

We have, however, indicated where American assumptions, expectations, and behavior may be different to common tendencies elsewhere in the world.

WHERE DO I GO FROM HERE? – MANAGEMENT AND TEAMWORK WITH AMERICANS

"So if I am managing a group or leading a team of Americans, and want to avoid and prevent the behavior we have seen in the example, what do I do?"

How Americans view foreign management

At this point, you may have found very little that is culturally shocking, new, or even very different to preferred management practices where you come from. That should not surprise us, given the increasingly international language of management. Alternatively, you may have found aspects of the American way that are different from what you are accustomed to, and what you are comfortable with. Whatever differences you may see in this area, it is worth remembering that Americans may *perceive you as different*, based on their images of and experiences with non-American management. Box 6.5 lists a number of these American perceptions.

Box 6.5: American perceptions

European managers: Not entrepreneurial
Not focused on the customers
Too cautious; will not take risks

Japanese managers: Too slow
No decision-makers; can't say "no"

German managers: Too technical
Not commercial
Inflexible

Asian managers: Poor communicators, do not get to the point

British managers: Don't tell you where you stand
Poor at dealing with women

African managers: Not loyal to the company
Not in control

French managers: Too concerned with rank
Too theoretical, not practical
Argumentative, negative

Mexican managers: Too slow, not prepared

Are these perceptions out-of-date? Perhaps. Are they too subjective? Of course. Too negative? Definitely. Americans have positive impressions as well, but those are not the ones that may interfere with your relationship.

But are they wrong? Maybe or maybe not, but these perceptions will influence an American's expectations of a non-American boss. For that reason alone, if you are managing Americans (or a group that includes Americans) it is important to approach the task thoughtfully, aware of possible differences.

What is the best management style to use with Americans?

As we noted earlier, this will depend on the people and the situation, and you will need to be flexible. We can certainly offer several guidelines, which will be applicable to you according to your background and situation.

♦ Do not expect in any way to be someone's boss away from work.

♦ Do not regard yourself as a kind of "parent", responsible for or having any obligation regarding an employee's personal problems.

♦ Focus on individual performance – goals, objectives, skills – as much as on team performance. Remember, your "direct report" is looking to establish a visible record of specific achievement.

♦ Do not assume, "They are professionals; they know when they've done a good job. I don't need to tell them." Many Americans want their work to be noticed by management. You will need to reach a balance between their needs for both recognition and autonomy.

♦ Be absolutely clear in communicating your requirements and expectations. Americans will expect you to lead as well as manage. They expect new managers from executive level down to supervisory level to want to make changes.

♦ If you have a different view on why and how meetings should be conducted, then you must be very clear as to what you expect and *why*. If you want to promote wider participation, greater discussion of problems, or more group consultation, then say so. Explain precisely how you want meetings or tele-conferences (or video-conferences) to be conducted. Americans will accept and support that. Remember – they will make conscious efforts to adopt the behavior needed to get the job done. You're the manager, and your American team expects you to indicate what you expect.

◆ Let them know where they stand. Your American direct reports may or may not like you, but they do respect your role, and its impact on their performance and development.

What style of management can I expect from an American boss?

While we cannot make predictions, here are a few things you might find in comparison to what you may be used to:

◆ "Aggressive" individual targets, in measureable terms. Many of those individual targets will in turn serve as group objectives for your direct reports.

◆ A fairly wide range of authority delegated to you, both for business decisions in your function, and for hiring (and, yes, firing), training and promoting staff.

◆ An expectation that you will keep your American boss fully and rapidly informed.

You are, after all, a "direct report". Your boss wants no surprises, and needs to be able to respond when his boss in turn asks for a report. Two good "rules of thumb" here are: (1) **When**

in doubt, over-inform. (2) When asked for information that you do not have, do *not* say, "I don't know." Say, "I'll check on that and get back to you."

◆ An expectation that you will show that "disagree but commit" spirit that we described earlier.

If you must disagree, offer a better idea. Criticisms should be formulated into specific recommendations for improvement. Another rule of thumb: **Never a problem without a solution.**

You may have noted that several items on the list of American perceptions have to do with communication. Whether your dealings with Americans are in the role of customer, supplier, manager or team member, your abilities to communicate with them will have the biggest impact on you success. Let us look at the subject in more detail.

Business Communication, American Style

The American at heart is a salesperson, committed to convincing others of his or her own point of view.

E. C. Stewart and M. J. Bennett[1]

The way Americans communicate with each other in business reflects both the social needs that we discussed in Chapter 4, and the particular demands of business situations. Can we describe a particularly American way of communicating, an American "comfort zone" in communication? Yes we can, if we understand that, as with any of our generalizations, each individual American will differ in some respects.

In this chapter, we look at the most important characteristics of this style, what these characteristics mean to Americans, and how Americans may react to others who have a different approach.

You can then begin to compare your own style, your "comfort zone", with what Americans are used to and expect from others. This in turn will help you:

(1) To understand why Americans may respond to you in a particular way;

(2) To see how you can modify your style to be more effective in communicating with Americans, whether in explaining, requesting, persuading, proposing or negotiating.

Simply speaking good English will help, but it will not be enough. The question of language, however, is a good place to begin.

DO YOU SPEAK AMERICAN? – THE ENGLISH LANGUAGE IN THE USA

Our discussion of business communication with Americans starts with the obvious: English is the language of business, and the native language of the majority of us Americans. We assume that everyone in business speaks it as well. Our American education system does not attach a high priority to learning foreign languages, although there are ample opportunities to do so. A great many of us grow up, or indeed live our entire lives, without ever needing to speak another language. Our ear is so tuned to American English that we are not accustomed to hearing strongly accented English (with the milder exceptions of the American South, and some of our British friends). We do not generally appreciate sub-titled films or those that are "dubbed" (voiced over) into English.

Learning a "foreign" language

On the other hand, there are many Americans who do learn a foreign language to a very high level, because they cannot function in the USA without it. That foreign language is – English. Many thousands of non-English speakers emigrate to America each year. If you have spent time in the southern tier of the USA from Florida, across Texas and the southwestern states to California, or in the larger cities of the Northeast, you have probably heard Spanish spoken by local people. If you are going to be living in those areas, especially in Texas or southern California, it will do you no harm to learn some Spanish (unless of course, you already speak it!).

In the USA, you will find speakers not only of Spanish, but also of almost of every other living language. Where there are large concentrations of non-English speakers, government agencies will publish documents, notices, and forms in the languages spoken by those groups, such as – in addition to Spanish – Chinese, Vietnamese, Arabic, and Korean, to name but a few.

American English

But with those exceptions, American English is the language you will be hearing. If you are a non-native speaker yourself, Americans will appreciate your ability to speak English, and may regret their lack of foreign language skill. They may not, however, make any concessions to your abilities to understand them, either in the speed with which they speak, or in the expressions they use. American business English is not *significantly* different from the Standard English spoken in Great Britain, Australia, New Zealand, Canada, and other former British dominions. Note the emphasis. There are well-documented variations in vocabulary and usage, which can at times affect comprehension. But what is remarkable is not the variation; it is the fundamental similarity.

The American English you hear and read in business nevertheless has particular characteristics. It is a strange mix of punchy directness and soft imprecise cliché. It changes quickly in response to political, social, commercial, and technological trends and developments. New words and phrases, constantly created, pass quickly into everyday usage, despite the regrets of those who would like to see a sharper and richer language. As recently as 1994, an excellent book on business writing listed *e-mail* and *sound bite* as terms to "avoid or consider carefully" when using.[2] Both are now part of current business-speak – in America and around the world. I know no one who "avoids" or "considers them carefully" before using!

It is not within our scope here (a good example of business-speak, which actually means "We will not") to provide a glossary of American idioms, slang, and new terms. If you are going to be living in America, you will find it helpful to have a good dictionary or phrasebook of American English, even if you come from a country where a more "civilized" version of English is spoken.[3]

We would, however, like to indicate here two areas of difficulty in American business English that are rooted in American culture. The first is the use of metaphors and other figures of speech drawn from American sports. The second is the matter of sexism in vocabulary, grammar, and usage.

Playing hardball: sports terms in American business language

Many common expressions originate in the three most popular spectator sports in America: baseball, basketball, and American football. Even if you are familiar with these sports, you may not be ready to hear them applied to everyday use in business, as in the examples that follow.

Play hardball. This means competing with all the skills, resources, and tactics that one has, without making any allowances for other people's needs or feelings. It is a baseball term, denoting the highly competitive standards of professional (Major) league baseball, which uses a hard tightly packed ball as compared to a non-professional game (or "amateur") in which a softer and larger ball is used. ("Softball" is played with all the fierce competition of the professional hardball game, and there are indeed professional associations in which the players are paid.)

We dropped the ball on this one. This is another baseball expression, best translated as: "We made a serious mistake" or "We failed to do what we were supposed to do." This refers to an error on the part of a fielder, who is normally supposed to catch or pick up the ball after it is thrown or struck without dropping it.

From American football comes the expression *Monday morning quarterback.* This is someone who has played no role in a situation, but who analyzes a failure after it has occurred and tells those involved what they should have done instead. The *quarterback* is the player who directs the team on the field, while Monday is the day after most professional matches take place.

An *end run,* is an attempt to achieve one's objective by means of an indirect approach, or by going around an obstacle instead of directly at it. In American football, a team may try to advance the ball by having a runner try to go around the opposing team's defense, rather than through it.

Basketball is certainly the most popular of these three American sports in Europe. It has given us phrases such as *slam dunk.* This is an exciting play in which the player with the ball avoids all defenders, leaps up to the basket, and emphatically thrusts the ball through it to score. "This presentation should be a slam dunk for you" means that the presentation will be a visible and easy success.

The above are a small sample. If you are able to get to know these sports, you can more easily enjoy them socially in America as spectator or participant with friends and colleagues. It will also help you understand their language.

Avoiding sexism in American English

Americans have taken particular care to ensure that sexual equality is codified in speech. For the non-American, understanding sports metaphors is a minor problem compared to the danger of appearing "insensitive" in both your speech and writing.

Here are a few guidelines to help to find your way through the minefield.

◆ When referring to a man and woman together in speech or letter, when using the male title Mr., you should always use the female title Ms. or Mrs. as well.

◆ Nouns denoting roles or occupations are neutral. American English has dropped feminine suffixes such as –*ess* from words of this type, and "neutered" others.

Here are a few examples:

◆ Use *server* instead of *waitress*, although *actress* still survives for some reason.

♦ The term *manageress*, common in Britain, is unknown in the USA. (It comes up as an error in my American English spellchecker!) Do not use it.

♦ The terms *salesperson, spokesperson*, and *chairperson* or *chair*, *chairwoman* should be used instead of *salesman*, etc., *even* when the person you are referring to is male. As an example, we have in this book used the term *businessperson* rather than *businessman*.

♦ Avoid using terms such as *man-hours* which, while not in fact referring to people at all, appear to exclude females. In this case, *hours of labor* or *hours of work* is better.

In Chapter 9, under the heading "workplace correctness", we have more to say about general behavior in this area.

Outside of work, you may not have to be so careful about this aspect of your language. In business situations, however, – and remember, these include socializing with colleagues away from the office – you must be attentive to this, because you risk causing offence.

With that brief look at language, let us now turn our attention to how Americans use their language.

AN AMERICAN'S CONVERSATIONAL COMFORT ZONE

Access – "staying in the loop"
We Americans may like our wide open spaces, but we don't want

to get lost in them. On both a social and business level, we try very hard to make and maintain connections with others and avoid isolation. All people do this to a greater or lesser extent; after all it's one of the reasons humans communicate in the first place.

If you recall our example of chatty Charlie on the long-distance flight, we can apply the same lesson to Americans at work: we feel a need to stay "in the loop". We want to be sure that we are not left out or isolated from people, information, or rumor. This need reveals itself frequently in what Americans expect from group meetings, described in Chapter 6, and in the extent to which people copy each other on e-mails, memos, and messages. When I copy you, I am usually expecting you to copy me. In this way, I feel that I am in the loop, even if I never read the copies you send me.

Americans talk a great deal about being "open" and "accessible", and "exchanging" information and ideas. Because of this, we expect openness and accessibility – or at least the appearance of it – in others. We are slightly suspicious of the person – American or not – who withholds information or who appears to withdraw or stand off from the flow of communication at work.

The importance of friendliness – "Have a great day!"
In an earlier chapter, we noted how many non-Americans, yourself perhaps included, perceive Americans as "friendly" or "chatty" and "superficial". This characteristic – however one judges it – finds its constant and continual expression in American business (and other) communication in the friendly, or even buoyant tone of daily speech.

There is of course much other communication that is angry, blunt, or aggressive, depending on the situation and the relationship. But – as we noted in Chapter 4 and will re-emphasize here – a certain degree of friendliness is important to Americans for several reasons. First, it is inclusive. Unlike people from other cultures, for example India or China, Americans do not vary their interpersonal approach much when talking with friends and family, compared to talking with a business colleague, hotel clerk, or customer. Remember Michelle, our friendly "server" in Chapter 4?

Second, a degree of friendliness puts everyone on an equal social level. That does not mean that everyone has the same importance *in a given business situation*, but the appearance of equality is vital.

Finally, to an American, a friendly tone conveys the right degree of personal interest, and the right amount of social distance (or closeness) between individuals, to allow a relationship to develop. The opposite of friendliness is this context is not unfriendliness or hostility, but coldness and indifference. We Americans are often uncomfortable when faced with someone who smiles little, stands or sits too far away, shakes hands weakly, or appears otherwise expressionless. The handshakes, smiles, first names, and friendly greetings are an American's way of saying, "By appearing to like you in this way, I show that I am willing to see if we can do business together."

Do not confuse this friendliness with a desire on the part of your American "friend" to get to know you "as a person" on some deeper level. Remember above all that your business relationship with an American customer, supplier, or colleague will be based on the business you can do together, not on how well you get to know each other.

Feedback and participative listening

EXAMPLE 7.1

An English woman was recounting to an American colleague at work a particular dramatic incident that had occurred to her over the weekend. As the English woman spoke, the American continually nodded her head, and frequently uttered expressions like "Yeah, right..." "Wow..." and "I see..." in response to further details about the incident.

Immediately afterward, when the two had separated, the English woman exclaimed, "It was hard talking to her. I couldn't handle so much feedback!"

What was it that caused the English woman to be somewhat put off by her colleague's short conversational interjections? The conversation was certainly friendly and the two women spoke the same language, but something just did not fit. The English woman's expectations of appropriate expressions of interest in a conversation clearly did not include those bits of speech coming from her "listener". And yet, most Americans in her position would not have been at all disconcerted by all that "feedback". They would have taken it as the common expression of polite interest that it was – in the American comfort zone – and would not have let it disrupt the flow of thought or talk.

As always, we must be cautious when generalizing about people's conversational and listening habits. These are expressions of individual personality, and so vary greatly from person to person. They may also vary from men to women. There are also some regional variations in this in the USA, between northeast and southwest. Furthermore, as strangers get to know and trust each other over time, they settle into a mutually comfortable style of taking turns in the conversation, and adapt to each other's way of speaking.

We do know, however, that groups of people differ in what is common and accepted conversational style. At the beginning of a relationship, as our little incident above shows, these differences can cause some discomfort. Because Americans are used to more of this "back-chat" in conversation, they may react negatively to those who do not provide this. German or Japanese people, for example, rarely exhibit this reflex. As a result, Americans sometimes perceive them as impassive, cold, or disinterested. When the lack of "feedback" from one participant is followed by silence when it is their turn, an American may experience some anxiety. Silence means uncertainty.

Many Americans in business have been trained in techniques of "active listening" – the techniques whereby a listener actively responds to a speaker at various times in a conversation with prompting ("Tell me more about your requirements...") or paraphrasing ("So what you're saying is that user testing will take at least three months...").

These are, of course, useful strategies, and by no means unique to the USA. We Americans may not always practise them, but we are used to them and are comfortable with a conversation style involving feedback from our listener(s). This applies not only to situations of one-to-one communication, but extends as well to more formal situations of presentations or conferences involving a group. A certain degree of participative listening and questioning, for clarification or to obtain more information, is expected.

But not every kind of listener or audience response is welcome to American ears. We are less comfortable with people whose feedback takes the form of quick and repeated "interruptions" to make a point or argue. We often find these characteristics in people from southern Europe, such as the French, Spanish, and Italians, as well as in some people from South and Central America.

Eye contact

A degree of direct eye contact is expected by Americans in both formal and informal dialogue. We are comfortable with more eye contact than are many people from the Philippines or Japan, and with less than many Arabs might be. Too little eye contact, and we may perceive the speaker or listener as hiding something or lacking in confidence; too much and we expect a challenge.

So what is "too much" or "too little"? That is impossible to measure, and as always individuals differ. There is no firm rule for getting this correct in your dealings with Americans. What we can say is if you are comfortable with a lot of eye contact, maintain that habit. If in your culture less eye contact seems more polite, try to make a bit more when addressing Americans. If that is difficult for you you can try looking at the other person's forehead or nose. In any case, do not constantly or continually look away or down.

Body language

What about physical contact – touching? You may have in your mind an image – or experience – of the back-slapping hand-shaking Yank. Although it may be exaggerated, there is a grain of truth in that impression. A friendly and constructive business conversation may conclude with a long handshake with the right, while the left hand is on your shoulder. Or your American friend may put his hand on your shoulder as you are about to part. If you're English, Indonesian, or Japanese this may seem excessive, but it is a way that Americans reaffirm the essentially friendly nature of your meeting. These gestures, however, are *not* signals of agreement.

You must also bear in mind that American women will *not* offer or expect the same degree of contact. A handshake of greeting, and one of good-bye are appropriate, nothing more.

How close should you sit or stand when conversing with an American? Here again different habits are found in different cultures. The American physical comfort zone for one-to-one conversation is around a meter to a meter and a half – the width of a desk with chairs, or a restaurant table.[4] Further away than that, and your American friend wonders if you really want to talk to him; closer than that and you are "in his face" – too intimate or too challenging. You cannot, of course, be expected to measure that distance in an actual situation; you will judge it for yourself. Indeed the physical environment of your interaction will influence how close you can or need to be to each other to be comfortable and to be heard.

"But I'm not like that!"

You may be asking yourself at this point, "Do I have to act like an American to communicate effectively with Americans?" The answer in this case is – partly. It is true that many of the elements of our own conversational style are so habitual, instinctive, and reflexive that changing them is difficult. Yet we are capable of modifying our style if we need to; within our own cultures each of us has learned to adapt our style when we are communicating with certain people or to meet certain needs.

COMMUNICATING CLEARLY AND PERSUASIVELY WITH AMERICANS

How you organize and structure your communication is just as important to an American as your friendliness, body language and responsiveness. You can have more control over this aspect of your communication style, provided that you have some idea of what that style is. How do you normally prefer to make your point? How do you generally organize your speech in order to make your request, present a recommendation, or state an opinion?

Use the chart in Figure 6.2 to informally assess your own communication style by circling or marking a number on the 1–5 scale for each dimension. By comparing your rating of your style with what Americans prefer, you will be able to see if there are differences that might cause misunderstanding or leave a poor impression on an American listener.

Let us now look at each of these five aspects of communication style in more detail.

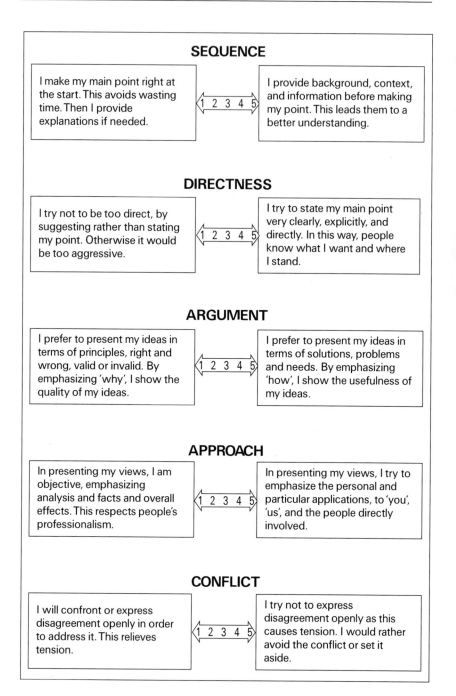

Figure 7.2. Communication Style Assessment.

Get to the point!

Consider the incident described in Example 7.3.

EXAMPLE 7.3

In a large American technology company, managers of the four key product groups were making their normal quarterly update presentations to senior management. One of these product group managers – relatively new to his position – was from Asia, although he had achieved his graduate degree and acquired his business experience in the USA.

During the quarter under review, his product group had performed well, and significantly better than the other three, so he had good news to communicate. He organized his presentation in two parts. In the first, he described the difficult business conditions that existed, the changes he had made in his organization and the lack of resources that he had had to face. With this as background, he then devoted the second part to a description of the very positive results that the group had achieved.

What is your assessment of this manager's approach?

◆ He is wasting their time. There is no need for him to describe what his group has achieved, since senior management would already be aware of it.

◆ His approach would be effective in helping senior management understand the reasons behind his actions and the group's success.

◆ He is too negative. He should make no mention of difficulties and problems. Furthermore he should spend time explaining how he will achieve even greater success in the next quarter.

◆ If senior management want an "update", then he has given them one that is complete and accurate, without boasting.

This approach made such a poor impression on his American audience that senior management began to question his fitness for the job. Before the next quarterly review, the Asian had been moved to another position in which he did not report to senior management.

Why? What went so badly wrong for him?

The biggest "mistake" the Asian made in this situation was to start off with the background factors. To him, this would have seemed an entirely professional approach, and one that in his culture would have been very appropriate. Perhaps your assessment was similar. But that did not work here. His American audience expected the "main point" at the start. His description of difficulties, intended to lead up to the discussion of results, was taken as a statement of his problems, almost as a list of complaints. That was not what they wanted to hear.

You may feel, understandably, that the management treated him harshly. But this unfortunate episode demonstrates the importance of knowing the "rules of the game" when it comes to communicating with senior management.

Most of all, Americans value a person's willingness to come to the point quickly. (If you are from northern Europe, you may also appreciate this quality, although you may not care for what you see as an American's over-enthusiasm.) If you appear to want to spend too much time "getting to know" them (in conversation) or discussing topics which seem off-track (in presentations), they first of all think you are wasting their time. Secondly, they may wonder why you delay getting to the point – Is it fear? or lack of confidence? Are you concealing something? This makes a bad impression on an American. Thirdly, as happened here, they may take your "background" as your main point, resulting in serious misunderstanding.

If you rated yourself on **Sequence** as 4 or 5, pay attention to this aspect of your communication style. Americans will generally respond better to someone at the other end of the scale. When you are meeting an American business partner for the first time, or approaching an American colleague in your organization, he will be most comfortable with this friendly, positive, and direct approach.

Be direct – s-p-e-l-l it out!

One perception that many non-Americans have is that Americans need to have everything clearly "spelled out" in communication. They often seem to be unable or unwilling to draw unstated conclusions or to understand what someone is "really" saying. There is a degree of truth in that view – In business, Americans need to know exactly what you need, what you are proposing, what you can and cannot do, as was illustrated in Example 4.4. You, on the other hand, may wish not to appear too aggressive or too demanding and may therefore be more comfortable expressing your position more indirectly. In that case, perhaps you rated yourself 1 or 2 on the dimension **Clarity**.

Mixed signals: yes or no?

When it comes to saying "yes" or "no", Americans sometimes appear to give mixed signals. During a meeting, for example, if a person makes a suggestion using a phrase like "Why don't we..." or "I think it would be good if...", an American might respond with "Great idea!" or "Sounds good..." Someone not used to American communication habits might conclude that the person is expressing support for the suggestion. In fact, the American may simply be adding to the friendly positive atmosphere by encouraging his colleague, but without making a specific commitment of support. Keep in mind that you are unlikely to hear a true "yes" (or "no") from an American unless he knows that there is **something very specific and clear being proposed or requested.**

Americans are not usually comfortable having to decode such expressions as "Don't you think you might want to..." (as a strong recommendation) or "Without some additional help on this project we will not be able to..." (as a polite request), or "That will be very difficult" (as a polite way of saying "no"). You need not fear being regarded as aggressive if you are direct. Your American colleague or partner will take that instead as a positive sign, that you know what you want.

You may even find it harder to say "no" if in your culture this can be regarded as disrespectful. Americans need to know where they stand with you, and unless they are familiar with other cultures in which direct refusal is bad form, they will assume that "yes" means "I agree" or "I will". They may not realize that you mean to say only "I understand". They will also assume that "That will be very difficult" means exactly that – there may be difficulties, but you will overcome obstacles and solve the problems. They may not recognize that you mean to communicate "no".

If this is awkward for you, find a way to say "no" in a friendly way, as in "I'm very sorry but we cannot agree to that" or "That will not work for us". Americans will understand.

Don't debate!

The pragmatic orientation of the American mind that we first described in Chapter 3, is first of all toward the application of knowledge and solution of problems. The Latin or Germanic mind, however, may often attach greater importance to determining what is correct, philosophically or technically. Americans are often impatient with what they see as the European's need to talk at great length about principles and rationale.

Americans do not care for that style, and are put off by the tone. To an American's ears, a German's willingness to say "That's wrong" is unnecessarily blunt. (Yes, we Americans like directness, but not harshness!).[5] The American is equally or more annoyed by a French person's apparent need to offer a *riposte* to almost any point that he tries to make in a discussion.

German and French people see this from the opposite perspective. Principles establish the basis for actions, while the "debate" is nothing more than professional expressions of clarity, attentiveness, and interest. The American, on the other hand, views this approach as too abstract, pointless, irrelevant, obstructive, and – as ever – a waste of time. The American wants to know not "Is it correct?" but "Will it work?"

There are, of course, occasions when Americans will adopt or respond to this approach, but it is not common. How did you rate yourself? If 1 or 2, Americans may perceive you as too analytical, too theoretical, too negative.

Approach – "What's in it for me?"

Project Manager Lars wants Sales Manager Jim to introduce a new billing system, developed at company headquarters in Switzerland, to customers in his region of the USA.

Version 1

"The new system will directly help the company's bottom line and will simplify administration across the board."

Lars   Jim

"That's all well and good, but ncreased sales will help)ottom line more, and for :hat I need *more* marketing)udget, not this. We should be focusing on simplifying the deal approval process, not billing."

Lars has tried a professional approach, but it is not convincing enough.

Version 2

Lars   Jim

"When your customers have implemented the new system your region will recognize the revenue more , quickly and your salespeople will receive their commission within 15 days."

"That means better results for our team, and happier salespeople. I'm interested."

Version 2 may appear to you as a clear case of good "selling," and would be effective with anyone. Perhaps. Viewed from a cultural perspective, however, America is a setting in which persuasion must be oriented primarily toward the needs of the individual that you are trying to persuade, not toward the good of the group, nor toward the logical validity of your argument. Americans regard the question "What's in it for me?" not as selfish, but as *self-interested.*

In this aspect of communication style, Americans like the best of both worlds. Facts, data, details, measurable results and other "objective" information are essential in any business case. Hunches, instincts, intuitions, or personal obligations are not compelling "drivers" to action. But data is not enough. Americans are looking for solutions to problems and the achievement of individual targets. Analysis is useful, but to persuade an American you must demonstrate measurable direct benefit to *his individual business goals.* This is naturally the case when selling to an American (or any other) customer, but it is essential when negotiating for resources or support *internally.*

In version 2, Lars has done just that. He made a proposal that helps meet Jim's objectives and addresses his concerns. If we set a rating on the scale for the most effective **approach** to Americans, it would be very near the middle. Americans want the data, but expect you to answer the question, "What's in it for me?"

Conflict

Handling conflict or disagreement is not easy, regardless of whom we are communicating with, or the language or style we are using. In the preferred American way, this aspect of communication is a matter of clarity and directness, our need to know where we stand. After all, if our goals in business communication are to achieve understanding, reach an agreement, and commit to action, conflicts or disagreements must be made clear and sorted out. Otherwise the path to action and outcome may be blocked. For this reason, Americans may become impatient or even suspicious if they feel that you are trying to avoid confronting a particular problem or issue.

At the same time, we have seen that Americans may be uncomfortable with blunt disagreement, or an argumentative or debating tone. We have also described (Chapter 6) how Americans may be somewhat more cautious when it comes to expressing disagreement or conflict in *certain* meetings. For now, however, we can summarize the American "comfort zone" this way: if you disagree over an important question, spell it out then and there, and offer a solution. Disagreements, in American business, do not interfere with personal relationships; they are separate from them. Even public disagreements, in front of others, are not likely to cause harm as there is no "honor" at stake. If your disagreement is on something that to the American is unimportant or irrelevant, set it aside and focus on what you are trying to achieve.

In short, Americans appreciate a style compatible with theirs, 1–3 on our **conflict** scale.

What can we learn from this?

If you have compared your style to that preferred by many American businesspeople, you may have found aspects in which there was a noticeable difference on our informal scale. Those differences are an indication of where and how you can adapt your approach to be more generally persuasive and effective with Americans.

If you found that your style closely matched American preferences, then focus on the final key to communicating with us: a positive attitude.

THE POWER OF A POSITIVE ATTITUDE

In your impressions of Americans, do you find us "enthusiastic" (good) or do you find that we do too much "cheerleading" (bad)? Do you find yourself sometimes distrusting this style? Do you suspect that the person may actually be concealing his lack of confidence, or weaknesses in his proposal? Or do you like this "can do" attitude? Either way, you have observed a quality that is essential in understanding the American way of communicating in business – the importance of expressing confidence.

Americans like to deal with people who appear to have confidence in themselves and their ideas. Expressing confidence shows us that you believe in your idea, that you "own" it, are in control, and take full responsibility for it. If the person speaking to us seems hesitant, tentative, or cautious, we become uncomfortable and may hesitate to offer support. "If you don't appear to be convinced of your idea, why should I be convinced?" Your confidence in communicating can be more important in persuading Americans to agree, buy, or respond than the actual business and technical details of your argument.

EXAMPLE 7.5

Consider these sets of statements, and how an American might react to each.

A foreign supplier is negotiating an agreement with an American buyer. He says to the American:

1)
"I don't know if we can deliver the quantity you need in three weeks. I'll have to check with operations."

Supplier   Buyer

"Sounds like he doesn't know his own operation, and will not be able to deliver."

2)
"I don't know if we can deliver the quantity you need in three weeks, but I'll find out from operations and get back to you."

Supplier   Buyer

"That's okay, but I can't aord to wait to find out."

3)
"We can deliver the quantity you need in three weeks. Just let me confirm that with my operations manager, and I'll get back to you by e-mail."

Supplier   Buyer

"He's willing to make a commitment, so we can do business."

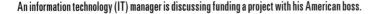

An information technology (IT) manager is discussing funding a project with his American boss.

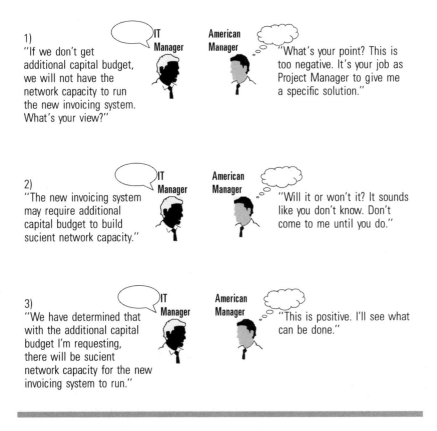

1)
IT Manager
"If we don't get additional capital budget, we will not have the network capacity to run the new invoicing system. What's your view?"

American Manager
"What's your point? This is too negative. It's your job as Project Manager to give me a specific solution."

2)
IT Manager
"The new invoicing system may require additional capital budget to build sucient network capacity."

American Manager
"Will it or won't it? It sounds like you don't know. Don't come to me until you do."

3)
IT Manager
"We have determined that with the additional capital budget I'm requesting, there will be sucient network capacity for the new invoicing system to run."

American Manager
"This is positive. I'll see what can be done."

Why would an American prefer version three in this case?

Be positive and optimistic

Like many competitive athletes, we "talk up" our possibilities for success – that helps to motivate us. We do recognize when someone is going too far – being too friendly, exaggerating the benefits or possibilities of success. But the American comfort zone accepts and encourages a greater degree of expressed confidence and enthusiasm than elsewhere. If you're Dutch or German, all this positive stuff may seem to you unprofessional, unnecessary, even naïve. If you're Japanese or Malay, the *individual* self-belief and control that an American expresses may seem completely inappropriate to the requirements of *group* effort. In any case, remember that Americans attach enormous importance to a positive attitude.

In both scenarios, you can see that American reacted best to approach **(3)**. In the first scenario, by the way, we are *not* suggesting that if you cannot agree to something or respond to a request that you should say "yes" and then "clarify" later. Being optimistic does not mean making false promises.

We Americans are by nature an optimistic people. Pessimism, doubt, or – worse – cynicism have no place where there's a job to be done. Show your confidence, your willingness to make a commitment, and then we know that you're motivated.

Play it up, not down

Making positive statements is good; making them in a positive *tone* is even better. You may make a clear and thorough business or technical case for your product or proposal, but if you communicate it in a tone that is too cool, too analytical, or ironic you may come across to your American friend as not committed to it, or somehow detached from it. Your American friend thinks to himself, "Where's the energy and drive? It doesn't sound like he buys into it." You can and should make those arguments without too much "cheerleading", but you need to show that you *care*.

EXAMPLE 7.6

A European country manager is presenting yearly sales results to his American boss.

Country Manager: *This slide lists the "second-rate"* [ironic tone] *companies that have become new customers in the past year.* [He lists a large number of well-known and financially strong organizations.]

Boss: *What did you mean by "second-rate"? Those aren't second-rate!*

C.M.: *I didn't mean they were second-rate. I actually meant that they were first-rate.*

Boss: *Then why didn't you say so?*

C.M.: *Since our competition is saying we're a second-rate supplier, I was just showing —*

Boss: [interrupts] *You should be less worried about the competition and more worried about how we're going to grow these accounts! See me after this meeting.*

C.M.: *Right*

Our European friend has run into trouble. His simple use of irony to make a point has failed, and instead has created an entirely new problem for him. His American boss is beginning to think that he is losing sight of the highest priority.

Do not downplay your company, your needs, and your accomplishments. If you appear to make jokes, ironic comments, or other remarks, however gentle or light-hearted, that seem to imply that your company is not the greatest organization on earth, you will most definitely turn off your American counterpart. You may feel that this attitude shows that you are relaxed, realistic, and credible. An American, on the other hand, may simply not understand your intent, or may hear this as evidence that you do not believe in what you are saying. At best he may think that you simply are trying to appear clever.

Many Americans will, of course, adopt a light-hearted, ironic, or even sarcastic tone when discussing business, but this will occur between people who know each other very well, who have a close collegial relationship, or who simply want to relieve tension or let off steam. Remember that in many situations most Americans regard this kind of tone as negative – unnecessary, irrelevant and ineffective.

So by all means, be friendly and relaxed. But save your jokes and wit for subjects outside business. (Even then you need to be careful, as we shall see in Chapter 9.)

SUMMARY – STRATEGIES FOR BEING CLEAR AND PERSUASIVE WITH AMERICANS

Keep people in the loop and be accessible
This is a factor that will affect so many of your dealings with Americans, and we have more to say about it in Chapters 6 and 10. We summarize it here by saying: take the initiative to communicate – with customers, managers, and direct reports.

Naturally, you need not add to information overload by sending out useless reports and e-mail messages (which many Americans do). Over time, you will get to know other people's particular requirements and concerns, and you can adapt the flow and frequency accordingly. It is essential, however, that you take a proactive approach: in working with Americans it is far better to provide too much information than too little.

Allow yourself to be (or appear to be) accessible to all Americans with whom you have direct dealings, regardless of their level of responsibility. They may not try to contact you directly, but they want to feel as if they can.

Treat American women in the same way as you do men!

Do not vary your communication style when addressing American businesswomen as compared to addressing men. A handshake as greeting, using first names, and all aspects of your speech style should be consistent. Leave out the backslap...

Do not, in your communication, call attention to the fact that you are addressing or referring to a woman.

Get to the point and spell it out

Be prepared to get down to business quickly. Spell out precisely what you need, offer, or propose. Only then will you obtain a real agreement – a kind of informal contract – from an American. ("If you're ever in Dayton, Ohio...") "Yes" means *yes* when there is something specific to be done.

If you wish to criticize, offer a better idea

Americans will receive your disagreement and criticism better if you offer a solution. They will be very impatient if you put things in terms of "right and wrong", but will have a more open mind if you state things in terms of problems and solutions.

Remember that American senior management does not expect you to bring your problems to them, unless you have solutions to recommend. At that point, they can exercise their power of approval or rejection.

Sell your ideas

When seeking resources and co-operation from American colleagues or managers, *present* your proposal/request almost as if you were addressing a customer. Direct the conversation, state your objective, and use a short agenda, summaries and other techniques. American business communication is itself a kind of commercial transaction: you "own" the objective; you are "selling" your point of view; you want "buy-in".

This sends out good signals to an American businessperson – confidence, readiness to get down to business, and a "can-do" attitude.

8

"Let's Make a Deal!": Negotiating with Americans

Negotiating is a specific type of communication with its own particular characteristics and challenges, and for that reason we consider it separately.

In the previous chapter, we described American business communication styles, and recommended certain approaches for being persuasive with Americans. In those situations, your goals are to influence your American partners and colleagues, to enable them to see your point of view, and to be clear and credible.

Since negotiation is a process in which two or more parties try to reach agreement on some kind of exchange, it is different from "selling" or persuasion. In the latter case, one party is simply trying to *convince* another to agree, to accept, to authorize, or to buy according to stated conditions. There is no exchange or trade-off involved. In negotiation, on the other hand, participants are trying to maximize the benefit for themselves and their organizations, of that exchange by relying on either power or trust. This presents a crucial strategic choice to every negotiator.

YOUR CHOICE – POWER OR TRUST?

Every negotiation involves power and trust to a degree, but the relative weight attached to one or the other depends in part on the desired relationship. If one side intends to establish a long-term, mutually beneficial partnership with the other, then advantage can be best obtained by negotiating so as to ensure trust, clarity, and mutual understanding. On the other side of the coin may be a desire to maximize short-term gains and mutual independence. In that case, parties in the negotiation may choose instead to emphasize their power. One way of doing that is to communicate so as to be deliberately ambiguous, to conceal one's feelings and real objectives, or to cause anxiety in the others involved.

Therefore when negotiating with Americans, you may *not* want to communicate in a way with which they are comfortable. For very sound business reasons, you may instead want to cause them to feel uncomfortable and more anxious so that their position is weakened. To achieve this, you may want to exhibit certain elements of communication style in a very different manner to that suggested in Chapter 7. It may be to your advantage to appear impassive and unenthusiastic; to take a long time in getting down to business in the negotiation; or to argue over principles or seemingly irrelevant matters such as where people sit. *Aspects of your communication style that may hinder your ability to be clear and persuasive in other dealings with Americans may be effective tactics when it comes to negotiating.*

It is not our purpose here to teach you negotiation skills and tactics. Skilled negotiators understand that both approaches – the power-based "pure bargaining" and the trust-based "joint problem-solving"[1] – need to be brought into every negotiation, and they know how to manage the tension between the two. Your choice between the two is sometimes limited by situational factors. As a buyer or seller, you have more independence and thus more latitude in that choice than if, for example, you are "negotiating" your performance targets and objectives with your American boss.

We simply want to remind you of the choice that is there. If you understand how Americans view and approach negotiation situations, you will have a sounder basis for making that strategic choice.

Before going further, however, we ought to point out that negotiation is one area of business in which Americans are very aware of international differences. Dealing with Arab organizations in the 1970s and early 80s, and Japanese organizations in recent years have taught them that "foreigners" negotiate not only differently, but also effectively. Many hard lessons were learned from those contacts.

So what, then, is the American way of negotiation?

SELF-INTEREST AND CO-OPERATION

We Americans first, and above all, make the pragmatic assumption that in a negotiation, both parties are trying to maximize benefits to their organizations as far as possible. Furthermore, we expect that each side will look out for its own interests: you look after yours, I look after mine. This is not to say that we do not co-operate; both parties are to some degree interdependent and need each other. Otherwise they would not be negotiating. But any agreement we reach will be based on self-interest, a further reflection of our attitudes toward organization and teamwork that we described in Chapter 6.

A contrast with Japan illustrates this point. Management writers have observed on a very different assumption that has characterized negotiations between Japanese companies. A subcontractor who is absolutely dependent on a large customer for survival is in a weak position. The customer recognizes this, and will feel obligated to a degree to look after its supplier. (I will leave it to our Japanese readers to decide if that assessment is still applicable.)

In the American view, a seller may perceive a buyer as being in the stronger position, but the seller does not expect to be taken care of or looked after by the buyer. The buyer, in turn, does not expect to have to look after the interests of the seller in any way. Weak or strong, each side retains its independence, and looks after itself. The "obligations" of each are specified in the written contract. It is in the contract, the law, not in the obligations of their relationship, that each side finds its protection. This, to an American, represents a "fair" and "co-operative" agreement. Fairness does not mean equality of outcome, nor does it oblige the more powerful side to help the weaker.

At the same time, we also believe (or like to think that we believe) that it is possible to achieve this competitive outcome under the idealistic slogan of "win-win". The objective of the negotiation process is *not* to find the perfect logical solution, the objectively "right" one. It is instead to reach an agreement of maximum benefit to your side, which both sides can "feel good about".

WHAT'S NEGOTIABLE?

EXAMPLE 8.1

An American engineering consultancy has just signed a contract with a client in Turkey, which includes detailed provisions for scope of services, schedule, agreed price, quality specifications, and so on. The signing was celebrated with a splendid dinner in one of Ankara's best restaurants, for which the client paid, in the tradition of Turkish hospitality.

Work has begun, to this client's satisfaction, at a price agreed before the start of the work. Upon receipt of the invoice from the American company, the Turkish client asks for a further discount.

How do you view this?

a) It would depend to some extent on the reason for the request, but there is nothing wrong with asking for an additional discount.

b) One should always do this, and I would expect it.

c) The Turkish client is wrong to do this after a contract has been signed and agreed, and work has begun.

d) This is typical business behavior in some parts of the world.

e) It is a signal that the Turkish client is having problems in some part of its business.

The expectations of American business people in this regard correspond to those of businesspeople from many other countries, northern Europe especially, when it comes to contracts of purchase, sale, service, performance and so on. What is **not** negotiable is the terms of a contract once agreed, with the sole exception of a major crisis or impending disaster. Renegotiation does occur, but it is not expected, unless it is permitted under the terms of the agreement.

In the short case described above, many Americans would be surprised, frustrated, and upset by the client's "demand". Alternative **(c)** best decribes their reaction. More savvy American businesspeople might respond with a firm rejection, or a polite "Not at present, but we can consider that when looking at future business" or even a willingness to renegotiate certain terms of the contract. They won't like it, though. They might view this as suggested in alternative **(e)**, but only as an indication of major dissatisfaction with some aspect of the service being provided. This is not the case in this scenario.

You may come from a business culture in which it is more acceptable to propose a renegotiation of price or other terms, based on your relationship with your business partner or simply on the basis of a change in circumstances, as in alternatives **(a)** or **(b)**. To your way of thinking, the renegotiation may strengthen your relationship. Your American partner, however, may see it as evidence that you cannot be trusted, and as a weakening of your relationship.

This attitude will set the pattern for the whole negotiation. An American will expect in a negotiation that the other party will make their objections, complaints, and arguments *before* the contract is signed, not afterward. A negotiation is not just an indication of an intention to do business, nor a description of a "relationship". It sets out the "rules of the game", the contract, which will bind both parties.

"LET'S GET DOWN TO BUSINESS!" – HOW DO AMERICANS CONDUCT NEGOTIATIONS?

The following example illustrates a number of aspects of the American way of negotiation.

EXAMPLE 8.2

A Chinese Managing Director, accompanied by his Financial Director and Production Manager, is visiting the USA to negotiate their annual sales contract with their biggest American customer.

The visitors have spent an enjoyable and friendly afternoon on the golf course with their American counterparts, who include the Purchasing Manager, the Quality Engineering Manager, and the Vice-president Asia-Pacific, whom they have known for two years. Not only did the visitors win; they spent an equally enjoyable evening together with their hosts at dinner.

Suppliers and customers – except for the Chinese Managing Director and the American Vice-president Asia Pacific, who are touring the plant – meet together the next morning to begin the negotiation. The Chinese are surprised to find themselves immediately presented with a detailed list of price, quantity, and quality demands that they will be totally unable to accept. What is more, they had previously communicated this position to the Americans when preparing for the negotiation.

Your view?

a) This shows typical American superficial friendliness. The Chinese will not trust them.

b) There should be nothing surprising about the American action. It is standard practice in important international negotiations, in America, China, and elsewhere.

c) The Americans are wrong to be so aggressive in their demands. This will not help their relationship with their Chinese supplier.

A relationship is good, a deal is better

The most basic American assumption here is that you are negotiating on behalf of your business or organization (even if you are an independent sole provider), and so the immediate personal relationship between the negotiators – although it may be useful for facilitating contact – has only limited importance. The personal relationship between the two of you, cemented on the golf course, over dinner, or with frequent contact over time, may serve to make negotiation easier but it will have no bearing on immediate business needs. If you responded **(a)** in Example 8.2, we would say that while the Chinese (or anyone) may react with mistrust, the Americans are acting on the basis that trust arises from the way you do business together, not from your relationship.

Each party has the authority to reach an agreement

Americans will further assume that you have full authority to conclude an agreement, and will be responsible for its implementation. American negotiators will have their specifically delegated authority, and will expect that you have yours. That gives each negotiator equal status in the negotiation. If you have to continually consult higher levels of management for approval, sooner or later your American counterpart will conclude that he is wasting his time negotiating with you.

The American also assumes, unless it is clearly understood otherwise, that you are will be negotiating the details *there and then*. He will not usually appreciate an approach whereby you are only there to set the stage for "real" negotiations sometime later.

On the other hand, while you may need to consult your directors, Americans will not hesitate to consult their lawyers! This may annoy you, but it is not normally a sign of distrust or possible conflict. It is usually a positive sign: the American wants to know if he can legally agree to a particular item, so that it can be put into the contract.

Apart from the need to consult these other authorities, Americans will expect the negotiations to be carried on directly between the two parties. Certain issues or details can be left to designated subordinates or intermediaries, provided that the parties agree to this. If, however, other people are used as indirect lines of communication, Americans may see this not as good diplomacy, but as an attempt to avoid confronting an issue or to go behind one's back.

Team negotiations – everyone's a chief

When it comes to team negotiations, Americans very often expect each member of their team to speak for his particular function, requirements, and objectives. Each member will accordingly determine whether a proposal satisfactorily addresses his individual needs. Furthermore, they may expose their differences with each other publicly, in front of you.

To you this may seem like lack of coherence and discipline. To Americans, on the other hand, this signals openness, honesty, and "sharing". They will normally expect the same of your team, with people of both sides more or less freely expressing themselves to any other member of the other team. This is similar to common American behavior in most business meetings that have a specific objective. If you have something to say, you speak up. Silence means you have nothing to say. Consequently, Americans may not be used to hearing from or addressing a single "chief" or designated spokesperson.

What do we talk about? When?

The fundamental American approach to the actual negotiation itself will focus on resolving and deciding, not debating. Americans are likely to prefer:

1. To **start discussing specific issues quickly**, without spending time discussing principles, preliminaries, the order of issues to be negotiated, the setting of the negotiation, or the "shape of the table". In Example 8.2, they have signalled this clearly to their Chinese suppliers.

2. To adopt a correspondingly **narrow focus on specific outcomes**, what is to be done or delivered by whom, when, where, how, and for how much. Depending on what you are accustomed to in your country, you may be surprised that American negotiators at fairly high levels will want to negotiate details, rather than expect more junior people to handle them.

Americans may also not be satisfied with "agreements in principle". To a British management consulting firm, for example, this may be a valid way to establish a commercial relationship wherein the exact requirements and services will be determined as the need arises. Americans may show a much greater insistence on specific and detailed provisions from the start. To the British negotiator, the American is inflexible. To the American, the "Brit" is being vague and non-committal.

3. To follow a more or less **linear progression of discussion**, according to an agenda agreed beforehand or at the time. Once a particular point has been dealt with, there should be no need to return to it, except as summary and confirmation (or in case of clearly signalled need).

Experienced American negotiators are flexible in the strategies and approaches that they adopt, and recognize these when others employ them. Those who are less experienced, however, may become frustrated and impatient with those on the other side of the table who do not meet their expectations:

♦ A supplier from Chile who makes a long introductory statement concerning his organization, its history, and product range;

♦ A French Directeur who explains to his American Finance Vice President the particular needs of the French market and suggests that his Accounting Manager be the one to handle the request;

♦ An Egyptian Information Technology Manager who appears to

want to go back over issues already discussed and then to skip over other issues on the agenda;

When those others are non-Americans (who perhaps speak less than perfect American English), the frustration and tension may be more intense...

"But you said an hour ago that you could deliver in 60 days. Now you're telling us something different...!"

"But I thought we agreed that already?!?!"

Those are the signs of an American who is losing his patience.

COMMUNICATION STYLE IN NEGOTIATING

In the previous chapter on communication, we described an American's "comfort zone" – the habits of speech, interaction, and non-verbal signals with which Americans are accustomed to conduct their spoken communication. Several of them need re-emphasis here, in the context of direct business negotiations.

Informal

The Americans will want to lessen the social distance by calling you by your first name, unless there is a very senior person present on your side, or unless they have been told otherwise. They will speak to "you" as if addressing only you, as an individual. If you are more comfortable referring to yourself in the negotiation as "our company", and to the Americans on the other side as "your company", this may be awkward. You need not worry – the Americans are addressing you as the *representative* of your organization.

Friendly

We have already seen how American friendliness implies few obligations, while facilitating social and business relationships. Americans view the negotiations as a process of reaching an agreement under "adversarial" conditions. By adversaries, we do not mean enemies, we mean people whose interests will conflict, but who need to find a way to co-operate. Since friendliness helps make that possible, Americans are comfortable conducting business negotiations in that sort of atmosphere.

Do not be surprised to find that even high-level negotiations are conducted under this friendly blanket, while the substance of the talks involves aggressive demands and blunt rejections. In Example 8.2, the American demands will no doubt be expressed in this friendly way, with further small talk about the golf game and the dinner. Lack of friendliness implies "keeping your distance", which an American may in turn interpret as an unwillingness to do business, caution, or even evasiveness.

Americans love to use very positive and encouraging terms such, as "win-win" or "partnership" (especially if they are a supplier or potential supplier) to describe the outcome they desire. But they will be looking for a rapid agreement that will meet their objectives. Whether that agreement meets your objectives is your responsibility. Americans will compromise, but they do not regard compromise as an ideal outcome, unlike many negotiators from, say Britain, or northern Europe. "Win-win" might be better translated as, "I win; you think you've won" or "I win but don't feel bad about winning!"

Direct

Americans are accustomed to signalling disagreement or lack of acceptance by a clear "no" or with an appropriate phrase that expresses "no". They will expect the same from you. Consequently, they may have trouble interpreting more indirect ways of saying "no", such as changing the subject, saying "yes" without further commitments, or using a phrase, such as "That will be difficult for us", that avoids direct negation.

Do not be surprised to hear your American counterparts directly express their anger, impatience, frustration, or defensiveness. They will try to keep those under control, but will not hesitate to let their feelings be known. "No way!" is an emphatic rejection. "That proposal is crazy!" is even more emotionally direct. You should not take such expressiveness as rude, insulting, or as evidence of a loss of discipline on their part. We like to believe that our emotion is directed at the *idea, not at the person* presenting it. "Don't take it personally", we say. Americans will do their best to ensure that an emotional reaction passes quickly, otherwise it will interfere with the business at hand, and will – as ever – waste time. We will generally want to restore quickly the friendly atmosphere.

Reading conversational signals

In Chapter 7, we described American preferences for a certain type of body language and the correct physical distance. What is particularly important here is the matter of "turn-taking" – establishing a comfortable synchronization of speakers.

In a negotiation, Americans may well be annoyed by an opposing party who interrupts quickly and frequently, especially if they interrupt in order to reject or disagree.

At the same time, Americans (and we are not unique in this) are equally uncomfortable with the contrary response: the other party pauses for a long time before replying, or simply responds by saying nothing at all. In that case, an American negotiator may relieve his anxiety by continuing to speak. And as experienced negotiators know, the more you speak in a negotiation, the more likely you are to say something unwise.

Do not deceive yourself, however. Highly trained American negotiators are quite capable of establishing and maintaining the informal friendly atmosphere they like so much, while responding to the other side's "difficult" style with tough terms supported by (smiling) threats.

GETTING AGREEMENT – "WOULD YOU PUT THAT IN WRITING?"

The phrase "Would you put that in writing?" is a clear sign that an American negotiator is happy with a proposal that has been made, and is seeking a firm commitment. Americans are quicker than others to want to put things in writing. Verbal agreements have little legal force, and are not sufficiently "black and white". If the other side refuses or appears to hesitate, an American will understand them to be implying, "We are not confident" or "We did not really mean what we said." The willingness to "put it in writing" is evidence of trustworthiness.

When an American negotiator asks that of you, do not take it as an indication that they do not trust you. It is their way of saying,

"We are ready to accept that offer as part of the contract. Are you?" If your answer is "no" then you risk annoying your American counterparts unless you explain why, and keep the discussion focussed on what specifically you need so that you will be ready to sign.

If both parties are ready to agree in writing, it's time for the Americans to call on their lawyers to draw up the contract. When it comes to concluding a negotiation, spoken promises are not good enough.

THE INTERNATIONAL NEGOTIATOR'S OTHER CHOICE – RESPONDING TO DIFFERENCES

At the start of this chapter, we noted that when negotiating with Americans you have a strategic choice (as indeed does any negotiator at any time), depending on the situation and your relationship with them. If you accept that there are likely to be differences with your American counterparts, in some or all of the aspects of the negotiation process, you have several alternatives:

◆ You can ignore these cultural differences completely. You would then make your strategic choice of a "pure bargaining" or "joint problem-solving" approach as you would in any negotiation.

◆ You can choose to adopt a communication style with which Americans are comfortable, and thus appear to be more co-operative. In other words, you can try to be "more American" based on our description of American preferences and habits.

- You can take an approach based on your "comfort zone", your preferred style. If that style is one that may make Americans uncomfortable, so be it. That allows you to increase your advantage, although it may hinder co-operation.

- You can choose to negotiate these differences, by introducing them into the negotiation, as subjects to be discussed and agreed.

Let us look at each alternative in turn.

1. Ignore differences completely

There is nothing at all wrong with this. We said in Chapter 2, that differences between groups are important if we believe them to be. If you decide to disregard them, you will be able to focus on the specific people, organizations, and issues involved, without having to worry about interpreting "cultural" behavior. The parties involved, if they are experienced, skilful, and flexible, will establish a mutually compatible way of negotiating.

The danger here is that if negotiations between your side and the American side break down, each may blame the other (which is normal) while at the same time making negative attributions about the other group: "Typical Americans – ignorant, inflexible, demanding ... can't trust them." Or "Typical Italians – argumentative, disorganized, can't pin them down ... can't trust them." We find that we are protecting ourselves by stereotyping others.

2. Adapt to the American style

If this alternative appears feasible and desirable to you, then perhaps you speak English fluently enough, and are already accustomed to dealing with Americans. Maybe you do this already – consciously or unconsciously – in your international negotiations. Indeed, many experienced negotiators have learned to modify their style to suit the expectations of the other party. Within this framework of a consciously American approach, you can then, of course, vary your tactics to obtain the outcome you seek. If communicating in the "American way" comes naturally, then it may be a suitable strategy for you.

There are some possible drawbacks with this approach, however. The first and most obvious is that it requires sufficient mastery of the English language to execute it.

Secondly, it represents, an initial "concession" on your part in the negotiation. By trying to adopt the American style, you are in effect negotiating on the Americans' terms, or "playing the game by their rules".

You will have to weigh those possible drawbacks against the likely benefits of having a better match of negotiating styles.

3. Employ a very different style, closer to your own, to gain advantage

We have mentioned several times how Americans can feel impatient, frustrated, or anxious when faced with a negotiation style that they cannot "read". An American negotiator with those feelings may be more likely to make quick, generous offers and concessions in order to get "the deal".

Therefore, if you wish to upset the Americans, or keep them "off balance", try these techniques:

◆ Delay. Take a lot of time before opening discussions or before discussing specifics.

◆ Start a long discussion of principles, history, and background before getting around to the detailed issues under negotiation.

◆ Keep saying that you have to "check with your boss" or "get approval from headquarters" before you can accept any such proposal.

◆ Keep returning to issues previously agreed, and re-open discussion.

◆ Say as little as possible. Remain silent. Pause for long periods before speaking.

◆ Retain an impassive expression rather than a friendly or smiling one.

◆ In team negotiations, pursue a united strategy with a clear goal (or set of objectives) for your side and a single spokesperson.

There are others, which we will leave to your creativity and imagination. Keep in mind that skillful American negotiators will often try these tactics on each other.

This strategy too has some risks to weigh against potential gains.

It will not endear you to the Americans, and as we have said on a number of occasions, they may conclude that they cannot entirely trust you. It also runs the risk of causing the negotiations to break down completely, since every one of these signals (except the last) can be interpreted by an American as, "I do not really want to do business with you."

4. Acknowledge and discuss possible differences openly

In this way, each party tries to understand more clearly where the other "is coming from", in the expectation that they will be able to trust and co-operate with each other more easily.

An example of this approach might sound like this, in which a non-American is addressing his American counterpart:

"Peter, I know that you would like to present your offer for technical support to our data centre, but before we get to that, we need to explain to you the development of our company's IT policy. In that way you can get a better picture of our needs."

If the speaker were very polite, he could add, "Is that okay with you?"

But, you say, surely that approach will annoy the Americans even more, in their impatience to get down to business.

To that we would reply, "Not really." As long as you explain clearly and specifically what you wish to talk about, and why, your American counterpart will consider it.

Another example might be:

"The agenda that you e-mailed to us is clear, but to us the issues are all connected, not separate. It will be easier for us in our discussion to consider them together. Then perhaps we can look at them one by one."

This is more reassuring to an American negotiator.

This strategy, however, is not easy to carry out. It requires first that you know enough about your own negotiating style to be able identify areas where it differs – culturally or individually – from the general American style. In addition, some differences are not really open to "negotiation" in this way. After all, you can't really say to an American, "The fact that in our culture we don't like to smile all the time does not mean that we don't like you..."

Nevertheless, this approach can help build trust and greater mutual understanding by admitting differences without concealing them, and recognizing that the other person may prefer another way. Whether these differences are based on culture, as some of them may be, or on organizational norms or individual preferences, making them part of your negotiation can strengthen your relationship.

In that spirit, we leave the choice of strategy for negotiating with Americans to you.

MANY EXCEPTIONS

Throughout our survey of American management, communication, and negotiation styles, we have suggested what American preferences might be, the sorts of expectations they might have, and examples of behavior that you might encounter. Negotiation is yet another of our gray areas, with many exceptions and variations according to individual personality, organizational norms, and situational requirements.

To set ourselves on firmer ground, let us now turn our attention to areas of American business practice in which specific guidelines, or indeed rules, can help you avoid certain problems and resolve others.

9

American Business Etiquette and "Workplace Correctness"

In this section, we take a short sharp look at important aspects of American business etiquette, and what we have chosen to call "workplace correctness". Etiquette is a matter of politeness and common practice. Correctness concerns itself with social politics, corporate policy, and even the law.

We have in previous chapters made a number of observations concerning common and accepted American practice with respect to home and business hospitality, and the proper forms of address for men and women. We will re-emphasize a number of those here and propose others in describing what is and is not accepted as appropriate workplace behavior. Some aspects of that behavior can have legal implications, which we will point out. We will not try to summarize American employment law, however, which is constantly evolving. It also varies from state to state, since much employment law is set by the individual states.

Whether your contact with Americans is as customer, supplier, colleague, or manager, in small companies or large, it will be helpful to be familiar with these principles and guidelines if you wish to avoid offending people, or even worse, finding yourself the subject of a harassment or discrimination complaint.

DRESS

In America and elsewhere, there is a trend toward greater informality of dress in the workplace. The extent of this, however, will depend both on the "culture" of the particular organization or industry sector and on the situation (customer meetings or more formal occasions).

Men: If you are a supplier, wear your tie and jacket, and look sharp. In the American business environment, making a fast positive first impression is vital, and people do judge by appearances. Go easy on the dark gray suit, however, unless you are a stockbroker. While this costume is much loved by our British friends, in America it is regarded as more appropriate for very senior executives, lawyers, and funeral directors.

Women: Starting in the 1980s, American women in business were advised to "dress for success". Reflecting both American "get ahead" ambition and the equality of the sexes, this advice set the tone for female dress at work – a generally conservative and understated suit or other ensemble, cut and accessorized to look both serious and fashionable. Here again there is considerable variation, depending on the industry sector, but American women, from senior management level to administrative assistant, will always aim for a professional look. If you are going to be working for an American corporation, take your cue from them, unless you truly wish to express your individuality by not conforming.

There are some mild regional differences in the USA with respect to business attire. In the northeast – New York, Boston, and nearby areas – people may more often dress with greater formality. In the South, the heat and humidity in the summer months invite a somewhat looser style; while on the west coast, people are generally more informal altogether.

The best policy for both men and women is a safe one – follow the lead of your co-workers. Otherwise (men), start with the basic tie and jacket, and then you can dress more informally according to the situation.

BUSINESS HOSPITALITY AND GIFT GIVING

This is an area of sensitivity for large American organizations, which normally have stated policies on what can or cannot be offered to or accepted from customers and suppliers.

Do not expect extensive gift giving for business purposes in America – policies of many companies severely restrict both giving and receiving. On a social level, as suggested in Chapter 4, it can create a sense of obligation that makes many Americans uncomfortable.

As part of your company's marketing, image, advertising, or branding, low-value give-away items are common, but count for very little. After you have a solid relationship with an American partner, then small gifts from your country or company are appropriate, though not essential, as goodwill gestures.

If you are a vendor/supplier, and invite an American client or prospective client to lunch or dinner, it is generally understood that you will pay. (See Chapter 4.)

Large-scale business hospitality in the USA, involving many guests, will, as in most other countries, be conducted as corporate marketing events. Contrary to custom in other places, however, alcoholic refreshments may not be offered. This owes less to the moral values of the company, and more to the fear of liability if someone drinks to excess and then does something stupid or criminal, or has a road accident on the way home.

WOMEN IN BUSINESS

> *If I were asked ... to what the singular prosperity and growing strength of that people [the Americans] ought mainly to be attributed, I should reply: To the superiority of their women.*
>
> Alexis de Tocqueville[1]

In the USA you are far more likely than elsewhere to meet women, superior or not, in middle and upper management positions.

As with men, you can in conversation and correspondence move quickly to first names. (See Chapter 4.) American women regard themselves as absolutely equal (or even superior) to men, fully capable of performing the same tasks and carrying out the same responsibilities. To call attention to the fact that someone is a woman is to set her apart. **Do not** refer to them, regardless of position, as "girls" or "ladies", however polite and flattering this may seem to you.

It is a good idea to use more inclusive language, as well, especially in the presence of women. If you are speaking of an unnamed indefinite person, use "he or she" or "him or her" together.

For example:

"Our new Marketing Communications Manager, whoever **he or she** may be, will be required to manage a budget of one million dollars."

Sometimes you will find this same usage in writing. We have not used it in this book, however, as explained in our introductory note. Over the course of a long document, such as a book or report, it interferes with smooth reading. In shorter documents such as letters or articles, however, using the pair of pronouns causes less difficulty. Americans will be expecting it. There is a growing if not quite correct, tendency in American business English to use "they" or "them" as the neutral third person singular pronoun.

With female customer or supplier representatives and colleagues alike, stay on a friendly professional level of conversation. Avoid commenting on or referring to someone's appearance, dress, or attractiveness. To many non-Americans, this would seem to inhibit relaxed communication between the sexes. In the highly sensitive American workplace, such comments may make a woman very uncomfortable.

HUMOR

Humor does not travel well, culturally speaking.

Be mindful of extreme sensitivity in the USA to attempts to show humor with jokes or clever comments that refer to someone's gender, religion, sexual lifestyle, or racial/national origin. These may or may not be funny, but they are very likely to cause embarrassment or offence in a business setting.

Do not joke, or appear to joke about your business, your organization, or your products/services, or any proposal that a colleague may put forth. It is likely to make a very bad impression on Americans, especially if one of them happens to be your boss!

HARASSMENT

Employees of American companies are considered to have the right to a workplace free from "harassment". Whether racial or sexual, harassment is defined as behavior at work – verbal, or physical – that is perceived by one or more persons as contributing to an intimidating or hostile work environment.[2] The exact legal definition does not concern us here, but the practical perception of it does.

Sexual harassment was originally described as behavior whereby a more powerful individual (usually a male manager) expected favors (usually of a sexual nature) from a less powerful person (usually a female) in exchange for special consideration or treatment. It has since acquired a much wider scope (same-sex harassment is possible) and definition. Sexual harassment may now include *any* persistent behavior of a sexual nature – words, gestures, repeated approaches, flirtations, jokes – which another person may regard as presumptuous, offensive, or simply inappropriate.

Apparently innocent comments you may make, or behavior towards others that in your country would be entirely permissible, may in America be regarded as offensive. Complaints about your behavior may follow, with great potential damage to your reputation.

Racial harassment is an offence that is analogous to sexual harassment, though largely limited to verbal expressions. Racist terms are the worst examples, but even terms that may be more teasing than abusive fall into this category. You should also avoid expressions that contain an implied racial stereotype, such as "Chinese whispers".

Keep in mind the following:

- Even if your contact with Americans is as representative of an external organization, you run the risk of ruining your business relationship or provoking complaints if you allow yourself, in dealing with people of the opposite sex, to go beyond the friendly professional approach mentioned before.

- As we noted in our comments on humor, avoid telling jokes that may poke fun, however affectionately, at other groups.

- If you are an employee of an American organization, especially in a managerial position, speak with your Human Resources person as soon as you can. Find out about company policies in this area. Whether you think that this matter of harassment is a contribution to a fairer workplace, or an over-reaction that makes relationships more difficult, do not ignore it. American companies are very anxious to avoid problems in this area. Being a foreigner, or someone for whom English is not the first language, will not protect you.

EMPLOYMENT PRACTICES AND LAW

This section will be particularly relevant if you will be taking a management position in an American company.

Interviewing

Another area in which American organizations are sensitive is that of illegal discrimination in hiring. If you recall the resume of our friend Lenore Madison, you may remember that it contained no reference to her age, race, religion, or marital status. In fact, she did not even mention the year of her BA degree, which would permit a reader to estimate her age (based the normal age of achieving this degree).

Why? There are two reasons.

First, as you might expect from what you now know about the American way of business, Lenore considers that these other items of data are completely irrelevant to her fitness for the job. Secondly, Lenore does not wish to make it easy for someone to reject her resume on the basis of age ("This job requires a young person"), marital status ("A married person is going to want to spend too much time at home" or conversely, "A married person would be better for the job, since she will be more stable and responsible"), race (so she sends no picture), or any other irrelevant factor. She will, of course, have difficulty concealing the fact that she is female.

This has implications for interviewing. Much of this personal data cannot be explicitly requested during an interview. (Some of it is, of course, visible.) If a factor such as age might affect a prospective employee's ability to do a job, then questions must be framed to focus on the job requirement, not on the age.

These remarks are merely signposts indicating where there may be pitfalls in American employment practices. These are hard enough for Americans to master, let alone non-Americans.

Again, your Human Resources specialist can advise you on the correct way of getting the information you need when interviewing American candidates for positions in your firm.

Conditions of employment

EXAMPLE 9.1

Alfredo is a manager concluding an interview with a candidate for a marketing position.

Alfredo: Lenore, it looks like we'll have a good fit between you, this job, and our organization! I'm willing to offer you the job now, with the starting salary that I mentioned. How does that sound, and when can you start with us?

Lenore Madison: It sounds great! I could start in three weeks, Alfredo.

Alfredo: That's excellent. I'll have HR prepare and send you an offer right away. See you then.

Two weeks later Lenore accepts an offer with a competitor, at a higher salary.

What is happening here?

a) Lenore has lied, and cannot be trusted. She gave a clear signal that she intends to accept the job on offer.

b) Lenore was giving a clear answer to Alfredo's question, but made no commitment: "can" does not mean "will". Afterward, she could still consider other offers.

Americans such as Lenore Madison, working at the professional/ managerial levels, do not always sign an actual contract of employment. Senior executives are the usual exception. It is common practice for such employees to sign an "offer letter", which states the position and starting compensation, but that may be the only formal signed document. Until that written agreement is made, the person you want to hire is not committed to your firm, even though you may have offered the job verbally. Lenore's apparent acceptance of the job does not bind her, and she keeps looking elsewhere (alternative b).

Alfredo should have tried to prevent this by keeping in direct contact with Lenore after the interview, in order to remind her of how much he and the company were looking forward to her joining them, and to respond in case she was thinking of changing her mind.

Once the person has "come on board", their conditions of employment consist of the company policies, procedures, benefits, and similar provisions that are specified in various documents, whether electronic or paper. They also include the job descriptions, stated performance expectations, and assessments of performance that are prepared by their management.

Consider the following exchange:

EXAMPLE 9.2

Manager: Jim, we have to make some changes to bring our department in line with the new strategic business unit. So you will no longer have responsibility for international accounts.

Jim: Just two months ago, you told me that you were planning to add two new accounts to my sector. Now I have nothing, just minor customers of no importance.

Manager: All our customers are important, Jim, and I did not –

Jim: [Sarcastic] Give me a break...

Manager: – did not promise that. Besides, things have changed since then.

Jim: You did say that. I have the e-mail to prove it.

Manager: I want you to plan a handover of your accounts in the next two weeks..

Jim walks away, and resigns a week later. He files a claim for "wrongful termination" (saying in effect that he was indirectly fired) and wins compensation.

Finally, as seen here, conditions of employment can include verbal statements made by an employee's manager on the subject of career development, new responsibilities, the possibility of promotion, and so on. In this example, Jim's manager has failed to understand this. His apparent promises to Jim of greater responsibility might have been intended as no more than expressions of encouragement and praise, but under American employment law in many states, these can in fact be considered "contractual" commitments made by the company.

You must therefore be very careful in what you say, orally and in writing, to the employees who report to you.

A question of rights

Our explanation of harassment and these examples of managers' mistakes in employment practice are not intended to frighten, but to warn.

American companies, as we noted in Chapter 6, are able to make reductions in staff relatively quickly and easily, in response to changing business conditions. But the individual employee has "rights" and protections that can make it difficult to dismiss him for anything other than misconduct or extremely poor performance.

In the private sector, at professional level, trade unions are relatively weak. As of 2001, less than 10 percent of workers employed in the private sector belonged to unions. There is no American equivalent to, for example, the German engineering union I G Metall. An American employee's rights and protections are primarily guaranteed not by union agreements, but by company policies, state and federal employment laws and, in the case of civil rights, by the US Constitution. You can't be much more American than that.

The Big Picture:
Preparing to Work with Americans

As we approach the conclusion of our survey of the American way of business, you may be thinking to yourself, "So what do I do next?" Or perhaps you've skipped over the preceding chapters and started with this one, hoping to find the "executive summary" so beloved by busy American businesspeople. Either way, this is the right moment to summarize our most important guidelines and recommendations on working with Americans and help you focus on putting them into practice.

Some of them will be more relevant to you than others, depending on your situation, your experience, and your objectives. Some of them may apply to working with almost anyone, not just Americans. But taken together, they describe an approach that is likely to prove effective.

WILL AMERICANS TRUST ME?

Any kind of close human relationship depends on trust; business is, of course, no exception. If you are unable to earn the trust of your American partners, colleagues, or friends, then all your efforts will come to nothing. Yet it should not be difficult to establish trust with Americans – we are after all an instinctively trusting people. Perhaps this stems from our naïve assumption that everyone is more or less like us. For that reason, you need to focus more on preserving the trust that is already present, rather than on trying to "create" trust through some sort of communication "technique" or cultural formula.

Consider these two situations.

EXAMPLE 10.1

Your company has acquired an American supplier, in order to obtain an important new technology that will give you a competitive edge in your product or service.

You have no intention of eliminating any American jobs, or even of replacing any of the American management, and will be undertaking a "strategic review" that will last three months. During the transition period, you simply expect the American organization to carry on more or less as before, and will announce any changes when and if there are to be any.

Is this approach reasonable? Efficient? Considerate? To you maybe, but not necessarily to the Americans, who may be thinking:

"Where do we stand in the new organization?"
"What opportunities will there be for us?"
"What changes will the new owners make?"
"With a foreign owner we will be cut out of the decision-making."
"With a foreign owner we will be far away and invisible."

... and so on.

Those highly mobile self-motivated American managers and professionals will have their resumes prepared and will immediately start to look over the fence to where "the grass is always greener". They will leave.

You are being sent to America for an indefinite time to take over the position of project manager of an important technical project, staffed by highly skilled American professionals. You are replacing the previous Project Manager, who left the company. You have been appointed because you are closely connected to the project sponsor at your headquarters, and can ensure that the project receives the attention and the resources that it needs.

At present, the project is progressing well. You had met the project team previously, and are on friendly terms with them. You have decided to delay your move to America for eight weeks in order to renegotiate the project budget with headquarters management, and to bring yourself up to speed on all the technical aspects of the project. You will rely on e-mails and teleconferences to keep track of developments in the States, and let the team carry on with their work.

What about this approach? Is it reasonable? Efficient? Respectful of the Americans' professional autonomy?

Maybe. But consider what the Americans may be thinking:

"Why did the company not promote one of our American team members to the post of Project Manager?"

"We are being managed at a distance, from a foreign country. How can they understand what is going on here?"

"We don't want him telling us how to do our jobs, but why does this new manager not get involved here?"

"Does this mean that the project is in trouble?"

... and so on.

You may have good answers to all their questions, but this may not be the moment to be "hands-off".

If you think that Americans have a tendency to take just this sort of approach when they manage their overseas projects, you now understand how they may be feeling in this situation.

Keeping the trust of Americans should not present a problem as long as you keep a few basic principles firmly in mind.

- In all situations, be ready to **"get down to business" quickly**. Americans want to get things done and avoid wasting time. This applies whether you are phoning one of your American colleagues to ask for information, leading a meeting of your American team, or making a sales call on a prospective American customer.

- It is probably safe to say that Americans are like most people in that they are inclined to trust people who express an interest in them, their needs, their goals. Do not be afraid to **ask direct questions** in order to find out what you can do for them.

◆ Adopt the practice of "over-informing" that we described in our chapters on management and communication. Or to put it more sensibly, make it a point to **keep people in the loop** – your American boss, your American direct reports, your American customers and suppliers.

We Americans are ourselves far from perfect in this area. Much of the talk in American organizations about the importance of being "open" is just empty talk. But it is fair to say that we do not trust people who appear to be holding back information for no good reason, or who cannot be bothered to communicate it clearly. There are at times good business reasons for holding back information, but there is no right of rank or privilege that entitles anyone to do so.

◆ **Be there. Be accessible.** When an American wants to talk to you, they want to talk to you *now*. Management, in America (as often elsewhere) wants answers to their questions *now*.

Americans do not always understand why their foreign partners or colleagues do not reply to their e-mail messages *now*. There are naturally several possible reasons for that: maybe your American friends have "forgotten about" the time difference between your locations. Maybe you are not the right person to receive the message. Maybe (usually?) you have more urgent matters to attend to. And maybe Americans would be shocked to know that their foreign and overseas colleagues make the same complaint about them! No matter. If you wish to preserve that trust, get back to them; talk to them.

There is another important reason to keep the principle of accessibility in mind in your dealings with Americans. If you are in a leadership or management role, accessibility means visibility. In Chapter 6 we saw how important this factor is to Americans in corporate life, and the clear impact of one's manager on it. But the consequences of not making yourself accessible to your people are likely to be worse for you. You will find yourself isolated, and regarded as someone who "hides behind his desk" or in their office. Keep in mind as well that making yourself available and accessible only to certain people will undermine the trust of the whole group.

American businesspeople themselves often violate these principles. But as a non-American, it is important for you to make a deliberate effort to put them into practice. Sensitive situations of international contact heighten the risks to you. Americans will not distrust you simply because you are a foreigner, but any apparent failure on your part to meet their expectations will be attributed to your "foreign-ness". A gap may appear that becomes harder to bridge as time goes on.

WILL I BE ABLE TO COMMUNICATE EFFECTIVELY WITH AMERICANS?

We have already described in some detail communication "American style" – the approach and attitude to which Americans are accustomed and with which they feel comfortable. We can sum it up by noting that your effectiveness in communicating with Americans in any role will be facilitated by these three elements:

- Your **friendly and confident tone**. Show that you like them, and that you believe in yourself, your idea, your product, and your company.

- Your **clarity** in stating what you want, what you can do, what you expect, what you offer.

- Your **persuasive approach**. Spell out the benefits to them of your offer, request, or recommendation. Do not be afraid to ask for a decision then and there on the next step.

Polish your horn, and get ready to blow it!

HOW CAN I ESTABLISH RELATIONSHIPS AND GET TO KNOW THEM?

Don't let yourself be frustrated by those quick and superficial contacts that Americans love to make. Take advantage of them.

- Be prepared for **networking**. Be ready to talk – at any moment – in concise positive terms about who you are and what you have to offer. This applies whether you are selling yourself for employment, your idea to your boss, or your product to a customer.

  Do not hesitate to network, if you think that a person you have met can be useful to you in your business. Whether or not you care to accept our friend Charlie's "If you're ever in Dayton..." invitation, you can certainly contact him after your flight if you want to pursue the contact for business reasons. Send an e-mail or phone him, saying how much you enjoyed your chat about quality assurance (or whatever). Then give him a reason to get back to you: ask a question, or offer to provide some information, for example. Take it from there. He would certainly do the same with you for similar reasons in the same circumstances.

♦ Use the various **organizations** we mentioned in Chapter 4 as opportunities for networking. Many of them are international, and will have branches in your country. Do not rely solely on trade shows, industry events, or professional associations, especially if you will be based in America for an extended period of time.

WILL AMERICANS ACCEPT ME AS THEIR MANAGER AND LEADER?

As we observed in Chapter 6, when it comes to managing Americans, there is no single model that will apply in all situations. There are certainly no simple solutions, no "silver bullets". Your experience and common sense will take you far.

It is vital, however, that you keep in mind those elements of management and teamwork that are likely to have the most positive impact on the Americans who report to you:

♦ You should develop a **direct interpersonal relationship with each individual**, "one-on-one" as we say. Much jargon – which comes and goes with fashion – has evolved to describe this relationship: "coach" or "management by walking around".

◆ Whatever you want to call it, just remember that there are two approaches your American direct reports won't want: they do not want a parental figure, not they do want to be neglected under the pretense of a "hands-off" approach. As time goes on, you will be able to get the balance right for each of the people in your group.

◆ Focus your role on **defining clear individual and group objectives**, outlining **clear responsibilities**, and providing the right amount of **feedback**. Your people need to know where they stand.

◆ In leading a team, show your **confidence and belief** (and, yes, even your enthusiasm) for the group's common objective. Your direct reports will know that many things you are asked to do by management seem unrealistic, pointless, or contrary to what they were asked to do last month. They do not expect you to be a cheerleader for management, but they do respond to a person who shows confidence and a positive attitude.

◆ If you are working in an American office, take the initiative to get to know your Human Resources (HR) Manager.

If you are going to be an expatriate in America, you will probably get to know the HR Department in any case, as the people responsible for the administrative aspects of your assignment. But you should use them as well for up-to-date advice and information on correct employment practices and other workplace issues. This is in order not only to avoid costly errors in behavior and practice; but also to ensure that you get assistance with the tools and systems that can make your job easier. If your organization does not have a Human Resources specialist, talk to corporate counsel (or in plainer language, the company lawyer).

ARE THERE REGIONAL DIFFERENCES WITHIN THE UNITED STATES?

The European traveller in America...is struck by two particularities: first, the extreme similarity of outlook in all parts of the United States (except the Old South), and secondly, the passionate desire of each locality to prove that it is peculiar and different from any other. The second of these is, of course, caused by the first.

Bertrand Russell, *Modern Homogeneity*, 1930

Americans might disagree with Russell, an Englishman. Outsiders, looking at any country or culture, see uniformity, whereas insiders, being more sensitive to the characteristics of the people around them, see differences.

This certainly has been true with respect to the "Old South" to which Russell refers. This region is traditionally defined as those states in the southeast of the country that made up the Confederate States during the American Civil War.[1] Up until 1865, this region had evolved a predominantly agricultural society based on a land-owning and slave-holding aristocracy. With the Confederate defeat, the economic and social foundations of that society were destroyed. What remained was deep animosity between many whites and blacks, great resentment toward the North (which was reciprocated with 100 years of contempt), a poor agrarian economy, and a distinctive way of speaking.

Southern middle- and upper-class values also persisted: the importance of "manners", loyalty to one's "own people", and a trust in one's word, one's *parole*, when it came to reaching agreement. In other words, these nineteenth century Southern values were very unlike those of twenty-first century American business. They implied a greater formality, slower pace of activity, and a much stronger sense of obligation.

Much has changed in America and in the South since then. The South has seen enormous economic growth, and much of the regional animosity has disappeared. So have the differences, some might say. But if your business takes you to the South, you may yet encounter people whose way of doing business betrays the lingering influence of these values.

As for other regions or states, market researchers can give you their analysis of differences. I can recall a marketing executive for a fast food chain telling me that they never test-marketed any new products in the New England states[2] because people there were too conservative, and reluctant to change their habits. How very un-American that sounds.

We should also add here a special word about Texas. It is the second biggest state in area (after Alaska) and in population (after California). It is the only state that was once an independent republic, commemorated by the "lone star" on the state flag. Texans do not hide their identification with their state, and continually express the idea that Texas is special. If your business takes you there, do not be surprised by this local chauvinism.

Despite these perceived differences, and the very real differences in demographic and economic characteristics between states, Bertrand Russell is largely correct – and *not* excepting the "old" South – when it comes to business. The mobility of Americans and the common characteristics of American organizations have tended to minimize – though not eliminate – regional differences in the aspects that we have covered.

WHAT ABOUT CANADA?

In your dealings with the people of North America, do not treat the USA and Canada as a single unit. The two countries may share the same telephone calling system, the same majority language, an enormous free trade area, and certain other visible features, but they are not at all identical.

Above all, do not refer to Canadians as Americans, even if you happen to come from "south of the border" and regard both peoples as *norteamericanos*. This is a basic courtesy, which your Canadian friends will appreciate. People from outside North America may have difficulty distinguishing the two when hearing the accent of native English speakers, and indeed people from the USA often are unable to tell the difference. There is a difference, but it will take time to attune your ear to it.

At this point, the best guideline we can offer is: if your business is likely to bring you into contact with both Canadians and Americans at the same time, try to find out beforehand or in your introductory small talk the nationalities of the others involved.

In Quebec, you may find yourself speaking English or French when doing business, but be aware of strict language laws designed to protect the use and expression of French. In many cases, you would be well advised to have your commercial documentation in French.

Having glanced at Canada, let us turn our attention back to the United States, and to preparing yourself for a successful short business trip.

PREPARING FOR THE VISIT

◆ When planning your itinerary, learn the geography in order to understand the distances and time zone differences that you will have to contend with. Americans may not do the same when visiting your country, but there is no reason for you to make the same mistake.

◆ Be fully informed of the American market for your products and services. That market is huge, but very segmented. If you propose to sell in America, you must also be aware of your competition – there will always be some – and of the national, state, and local laws and regulations pertaining to your business. Don't bother leaving home without researching all these areas.

◆ Make sure you bring with you something specific to offer or propose. Your American counterpart is generally not very interested in discussions "in principle".

◆ Ensure your colleagues back at your headquarters are ready to respond immediately to requests from you for approvals, support, and information. If you are going to the States to negotiate an agreement, be sure you have sufficient authority to conclude that agreement; your American counterpart will expect it.

♦ When arranging a meeting, it is useful to send ahead a short written statement of the objective and rough agenda of the meeting. That can be changed at the time and on the spot, but this preliminary plan will assure your American counterparts that you "mean business".

Are you are ready to do business the American way? Perhaps you have decided to adapt certain "American" approaches or styles to help you be more successful. Before you set out, however, as a final thought, it is worthwhile considering how you can enable Americans to better understand *your* way.

11

The Two-Way Bridge: Enabling Americans to Understand You

So far you've been reading this book in order, we hope, to understand more about the American way of doing business. You may also be thinking about how you can modify your approach to managing, communicating, building a team, and negotiating in order to be more successful with Americans.

THE CHALLENGE

You might also be asking yourself, "But what about *them*? Why aren't they learning about *my* country, *my* culture, and *our* way of doing business? Why don't they try to adapt *to us*?"

True international co-operation and teamwork are not one-way ideals. They cannot exist when only one party in a relationship tries to learn about and understand the other. Nor can they exist when people are convinced that there is only one way of conducting business.

Rather than look at this as a one-way problem, why not put the question to yourself – with a typically American positive attitude – as a two-way challenge:

◆ How can I, as a non-American, help Americans learn more about our way of doing business?

♦ How can I convince my American friends that other approaches to business can be equally valid or more effective in particular situations?

EDUCATING THE AMERICANS

The difficulty lies in overcoming the two obstacles of ignorance and scepticism in many Americans. In answer to the three key questions we posed in Chapter 2, many Americans would say:

"Yes, there probably are differences in the way people do business. But these differences are those between individual personalities and not 'cultures'."

"Countries may differ in language and customs, but people in business are basically similar. Any differences we have can be easily overcome in a friendly framework of common goals and clear rules. Look at the example (however imperfect) of the USA itself."

If you want to help them answer those questions differently, then you need to share your observations and perceptions with your American associates and colleagues. Use the questions in Box 11.1 to help you note down some of your observations.

Box 11.1

Questions to help you reflect on comparisons between America and your own country or business culture.

1. **Your perception of differences.** Refer back to your list of perceived characteristics of Americans in Chapter 2.

Have you modified this list in any way, based on the observations we have made here? Or have your perceptions been sharpened as a result?

Can you account for differences between American business values and behavior and those of your culture?

2. **What specifically would you like to tell your American friends about business values, attitudes, and behavior where you come from?**

3. **What would you tell the Americans about how to work more effectively *with you*?**

You may find it useful in addition to read what has been written about doing business with people from your country or culture. For example, if you are Arab or Chinese, companion volumes in this series which focus on the Arab world and China will give you an idea of the differences that others may see in your way of doing business.

All of these sources will help sharpen and balance your perceptions of differences (and similarities), while avoiding the needless stereotyping that inhibits real understanding.

The picture is not totally bleak. Many Americans are knowledgeable, and are learning from their international experiences. But many others can benefit from your knowledge and your perspective as a non-American.

Discuss your observations with your American friends. If they have had international business experience, invite them to talk about their impressions of business in other countries. While educating them, you will be establishing a dialogue that will in turn strengthen your business and social relationships.

> *Communication is facilitated when there is a willingness to express and accept differences.*
>
> F J Roethlisberger[1]

PERSUADING THE AMERICANS TO SEE THINGS YOUR WAY

I can hear you saying, "Education is one thing, but persuasion is quite another. Discussing cultural differences is a good start, and makes for interesting and enjoyable dinner conversation. But how do I persuade them to see our point of view, or to take a different approach in our multi-national dealings?"

Whether your contact with Americans is as a manager, supplier, colleague, or customer, achieving that goal will not happen overnight. Americans will not be persuaded by simple assertions that "Things are different where I come from." To many Americans, this may come across as defensive. They may think, "Why should they be?" or "So what?" Others may be politely interested, but not really convinced that they need to take these differences into account.

Your American friends need a reason to listen to you.

Dinner table conversation may provide an opening to this subject, through a friendly exchange of observations and experience. On sharper and more urgent business matters, however, you need to *sell* them on the idea. You will need to show them why a particular business matter ought to be handled in a particular way in your part of the world; why adapting to differences will help them attain a specific objective, realize a clear benefit, solve an identified problem. Remember – your American counterpart wants to know, above all, the answer to the question, "Does it work?" It is up to you to show him how.

What you have to offer as a non-American working with Americans cannot be measured in the commercial terms of buyer or seller. It is also much more than the fact that you are, or may be, different. What you have to offer is a different perspective on business problems, a new way of looking at things, new ideas, and alternative strategies for attaining business goals.

Do not be shy in expressing this. Take the initiative to talk to Americans about your perceived differences. Show them how these differences, far from being an obstacle, can in fact serve as a bridge to better co-operation and achievement. Be specific and spell it out. That's what Americans like to hear.

That way, they'll start building the bridge from their end, too.

Notes and References

Chapter 1

(1) This image first appeared in the USA during the 1960s in advertising designed to attract recruits to the Peace Corps. Its message emphasised the link between perception and attitude; if you regarded a glass of water as "half full", you had the qualities that the Peace Corps was seeking – optimism, and a focus on what could be gained. If, on the other hand, you saw it as half empty, you had a negative point of view, focussing instead on what had been lost. It has since become a common figure of speech, even a cliché, but it has lost none of its clarity.

Chapter 3

(1) M.R. Bellah, R. Bellah, W. Sullivan, A. Swindler, S. Tipton. *Habits of the Heart: Individualism and Commitment in American Life*, cited in E.C. Stewart and M.J. Bennett, *American Cultural Patterns: A Cross-Cultural Perspective* (Paris: Masson, 1995), p. 136.

(2) Cited in John Updike, "Whitman's Egotheism" in *Hugging the Shore* (New York: Vintage, 1984), p. 109.

Chapter 4

(1) Stewart and Bennett, ibid., pp. 92–93. We offer no comment concerning possible differences between men and women, since we are concerned here only with relative differences between Americans and other peoples.

Chapter 5

(1) Cited in "What Do You Think of the Rich?", *The American Enterprise*, July/August 2002.

Chapter 6

(1) "How TI Selects and Measures Managers, An address by J. Fred Bucy, Executive Vice-president, Texas Instruments Incorporated at the annual engineering honors banquet of Texas Tech University, April 1973". Printed article.

(2) Alexis de Tocqueville, *Democracy in America*, pt. I, chapter 18, cited in John Bartlett, *Familiar Quotations*, 14th ed. (Boston: Little, Brown and Company, 1968), p. 616b. See 'Recommended Reading'.

(3) G. Hofstede, "Motivation, Leadership, and Organization: Do American Theories Apply Abroad?", *Organizational Dynamics* (Summer 1980).

Chapter 7

(1) Stewart and Bennett, ibid., p. 145.

(2) Mary A. De Vries. *Internationally Yours: Writing and Communicating Successfully in Today's Global Marketplace.* (Boston: Houghton-Mifflin, 1984), pp. 319–338.

(3) If you are using an English word-processing program on your computer, one of its useful (or annoying, depending on your point of view) features will be a spelling check application based on American English. If your version is based on British English, adding the American feature will be useful if you are going to be producing many documents for American readers. (Canadian English spellings are closer to British versions.)

(4) To an American, this means from 39 to 59 inches (almost five feet). Americans know nothing about the metric system, be it a matter of length, volume, temperature, or weight. The exceptions are engineers, scientists, and runners – who know how long a 10k (kilometer) race is. The metric system is used in Canada however.

(5) Hans-Dieter Meyer, "The Cultural Gap in Long-Term International Work Groups: A German-American Case Study", *European Management Journal* 11,1 (1993): pp. 93–101.

Chapter 8

(1) Alan N. Schoonmaker, *Negotiate to Win: Gaining the Psychological Edge* (Englewood Cliffs, New Jersey: Prentice-Hall, 1989), Chapter 1.

Chapter 9

(1) Alexis de Tocqueville, *Democracy in America*, pt. II, bk. III, chapter 12, cited in John Bartlett. ibid., p. 617a.

(2) European readers will find almost identical wording in the Equal Treatment Revision Directive of 2001.

Chapter 10

(1) The states which seceded from the United States to form the Confederate States of America were, in order of secession: South Carolina, Mississippi, Florida, Alabama, Georgia, Louisiana, Texas, Virginia, Arkansas, Tennessee, North Carolina. West Virginia seceded in turn from Virginia in 1893 and rejoined the Union.

(2) The New England States are Connecticut, Maine, Massachusetts, New Hampshire, Rhode Island, and Vermont.

Chapter 11

(1) F. J. Roethlisberger, "Barriers to Communication between Men", in *The Use and Misuse of Language*, ed. S. I. Hayakawa (Greenwich, Conn.: Fawcett, 1962), p. 41.

It is a good thing for an uneducated man to read books of quotations.
Bartlett's Familiar Quotations *is an admirable work, and I studied*
it intently. The quotations when engraved upon the memory give
you good thoughts. They also make you anxious to read the
authors and look for more.

Winston Churchill

Recommended Reading

Bryson, Bill, *Made in America: An Informal History of the English Language in the United States*. New York: Avon, 1996.
A very good history of American culture and society as reflected in the development of the American language.

D'Iribarne, Philippe, *La Logique de l'Honneur: Gestion des Entreprises et Traditions Nationales*. Paris: Seuil, 1989.
Also published in English under the title of *The Logic of Honor*, this is an excellent comparative study of national differences in management, as seen in a comparison of three subsidiaries of a French multinational, in France, the USA, and the Netherlands.

De Tocqueville, Alexis, *De la Démocratie en Amérique: Les Grands Thèmes*. Paris: Gallimard, 1968.
Citations of De Tocqueville in the text have been taken from Bartlett for clarity of translation. I have in fact drawn on the above edition extensively as a 170 year-old validation and explanation of many perceptions and truths about American society in 2004.

Lawrence, Peter. Management in the USA. London: Sage Publications, 1996.
Written ten years ago, after a period of decline in American economic performance, this deep survey of American management attitudes and approaches attempts to offer an explanation for that decline and for a likely turn-around. While conditions have changed, Lawrence's description is very thorough and useful.

Mills, Steve, *Living and Working in America*. (6th edn.). Oxford: How To Books, 2004.

For the reader who will also need information on the practical aspects of daily living in the USA – immigration, banking, education, driving, and so on – this book is the answer. While written primarily for British readers, it will be useful to anyone.

Stewart, E.C. and Bennett, M.J., *American Cultural Patterns: A Cross-Cultural Perspective*. Paris: Masson, 1995.

A thorough description of American culture as seen from a social psychology perspective. Some of the authors' supporting examples are weak, but they do not detract from the strength of their analysis. (This edition in English was intended for French readers. The book was first published in the USA.)

Schoonmaker, Alan N. *Negotiate to Win: Gaining the Psychological Edge*. Englewood Cliffs, New Jersey: Prentice-Hall, 1989.

Recommended to any reader who wishes to learn more about negotiation in general, or American styles in particular. The author also makes some useful intercultural comparisons.

Whyte, William, *The Organization Man*. Harmondsworth, UK: Penguin, 1960.

A study of American society in the post-war years, a time when "alienation" and "conformity" were the twin preoccupations of American social scientists and social critics. Whyte is the former, rather than the latter, which gives his analysis a convincing balance. While written almost 50 years ago, it is a valuable guide to understanding the America of today.

Index

If you want to know how...

◆ To buy a home in the sun, and let it out
◆ To move overseas, and work well with the people who live there
◆ To get the job you want, in the career you like
◆ To plan a wedding, and make the Best Man's speech
◆ To build your own home, or manage a conversion
◆ To buy and sell houses, and make money from doing so
◆ To gain new skills and learning, at a later time in life
◆ To empower yourself, and improve your lifestyle
◆ To start your own business, and run it profitably
◆ To prepare for your retirement, and generate a pension
◆ To improve your English, or write a PhD
◆ To be a more effective manager, and a good communicator
◆ To write a book, and get it published

If you want to know how to do all these things and much, much more...

howtobooks

If you want to know how ... to communicate effectively with other cultures

'Doing business in another country is much more than flying out, staying in a posh hotel and eating different food. It's entering a different world, and you need to learn the rules. For that you need patience, preparation, an open mind and this book.'

Phillip Khan-Panni & Deborah Swallow

Communicating Across Cultures
Phillip Khan-Panni & Deborah Swallow

'A highly accessible and useful book that explains how to communicate with people of other nationalities. More than a book about body language, it explains how culture, values, awareness, respect and flexibility allow us to communicate effectively and without offence.' – Weekly Telegraph

'An excellent general introduction to communicating internationally. I particularly like the 10 top tips the authors give for each country.' – James Furnival, The Bookseller

ISBN 1 85703 799 5

If you want to know how ... to be an effective mentor

'Mentoring is an exclusive one-to-one relationship, is completely confidential and can be a useful complement to other staff development tools. This book explains what mentoring is ... and what it is not! It takes you stage by stage through the process and shows how it can be of benefit to and an opportunity for development, both for the person being mentored and for the mentor.'

David Kay and Roger Hinds

A Practical Guide to Mentoring
David Kay and Roger Hinds

'This book works through the process easily with simple steps and practical guidance, aided by an easy-to-follow contents section ... A handy and quick reference text for mentors.' Training Journal

ISBN 1 85703 812 6

If you want to know how ... to **get the most out of living in America**

'This book should not only be compulsory reading for those
planning or thinking about a permanent move to the USA, but
also for those considering a vacation or a teaching/lecturing
exchange.' – American Studies Resources Centre

Living & Working in America
The complete guide to a successful short, or long term stay
STEVE MILLS

'It has answers to everything you could possibly want to ask about
living and working in America, from visas and immigration,
employment and education, accommodation and healthcare, to
what life there is really like.' – Going USA

'The scope and presentation of the material is excellent, well
worth buying.' – Nexus Expatriate Magazine

ISBN 1 85703 913 0

If you want to know how ... to get a job in America

'... contains a wealth of information for anyone serious about making their living in the USA. The lists of major employers, recruitment agencies, newspapers, websites and other useful addresses are worth the cover price alone. A must buy for pond crossers everywhere.' – Pathfinder

Getting a Job in America
A step-by-step guide to finding work in the USA
ROGER JONES

'Essential for anyone who is thinking of working in the US.'
– Going USA

'... an excellent one-volume guide for those who still seek to work in the USA. Use this book to map out what is available, viable and within your grasp.' – American Studies Today

ISBN 1 85703 868 1

If you want to know how ... to present with power

'Your ability to communicate is the single most important factor in your professional tool bag. People who make a difference, who inspire others, who get promoted, are usually excellent communicators. The people who have shaped the course of history were all excellent communicators. They could move audiences, win minds and hearts and get people to take action.

The need to communicate is even greater in today's fast-changing workplace. Of all the ways you communicate, the one that gives you the greatest chance to make a powerful impact is the presentation.

This book covers all you need to know about researching your material, structuring your message and designing your visual aids, it also shows you ways to develop confidence and gives tips on how to deliver. Whether you are a novice speaker or a seasoned pro, this book will give you tips and techniques that will take you to the next level.'

Shay McConnon

Presenting with Power
Captivate, motivate, inspire and persuade
Shay McConnon

'Shay's raw talent together with his passion for the audience and his material make for a magical experience.' – *Siemens*

'His engaging style of presentation captivates his audience whatever their background or current state of motivation.' – *Director, Walkers Snack Foods*

ISBN 1 85703 815 0

If you want to know how ... to resolve conflict in the workplace

Margaret and Shay McConnon show you how to manage disagreements and develop trust and understanding. They enable us to begin meeting our needs and those of the other person, while maintaining the relationship and resolving our differences respectfully.

Resolving Conflict
Shay and Margaret McConnon

'One of the best books I have read on conflict resolution in my 30+ years in the field.' Mediation Office The World Bank

How To Books are available through all good bookshops, or you can order direct from us through Grantham Book Services.

Tel: +44 (0)1476 541080
Fax: +44 (0)1476 541061
Email: orders@gbs.tbs-ltd.co.uk

Or via our website

www.howtobooks.co.uk

To order via any of these methods please quote the title(s) of the book(s) and your credit card number together with its expiry date.

For further information about our books and catalogue, please contact:

How To Books
3 Newtec Place
Magdalen Road
Oxford OX4 1RE

Visit our web site at

www.howtobooks.co.uk

Or you can contact us by email at info@howtobooks.co.uk